Puppy Training in 10 Minutes a Day

A Guide for Busy People: How to Train Your Puppy in Minutes a Day with Minimal Stress

Contents

Introduction...1

   The Benefits of a Well-Trained Puppy 2

   What to Expect Along the Way................................3

   How to Incorporate Puppy Training into Your Busy
   Schedule...5

Chapter 1: Setting the Stage for Success.................8

   The Importance of Early Training...........................8

   Setting Realistic Goals 20

   Creating a Puppy-Friendly Environment 28

   Setting Up a Training Routine 34

   Crate Training Basics...41

   Investing in the Right Training Equipment...........47

   Using Technology to Your Advantage 54

   Creating Positive Reinforcement Systems..............62

Chapter 2: The Power of Short, Focused
Training Sessions...70

   The Science Behind Short Sessions 70

Timing and Frequency 76

Keeping It Fun and Engaging.................................83

Teaching 'Sit' 90

Teaching 'Stay' 96

Teaching 'Come' 102

Preventing Frustration for Both You and Your
Puppy 108

Avoiding Overtraining 115

Using Redirection Instead of Punishment 121

**Chapter 3: Training on the Go: Maximizing
Your Busy Schedule 128**

Training While Walking.......................................128

Training While Traveling or Running Errands....135

Training During Playtime 141

Involving the Whole Family in Training 149

Managing Training in Busy Households..............163

Using Treats Wisely 170

Using Praise and Affection...................................176

Rewarding Calm Behavior 183

Chapter 4: Troubleshooting and Maintaining Long-Term Success 191

Overcoming Distractions 191

Dealing with Setbacks............................198

Managing Behavior Issues
(e.g., Chewing, Barking) 205

Maintaining a 10-Minute Daily Routine.............212

Continuing Socialization.......................218

Celebrating Success................................225

Staying Motivated and Consistent........................231

Tracking Progress.................................236

Balancing Life and Training....................242

To Conclude Your Puppy Training Journey 249

References 253

Your Free Gift

As a way of saying thanks for your purchase, I'm offering an early copy of the book *Wagging Tails & Timeless Tales: 9 Touching Short Stories that Capture the Magic of Dogs – Through Joy, Loss and a Lifetime of Love* for **FREE** to my readers.

To get instant access just go to https://pawsitivepuppybooks.com/Puppy-Opt-in-Page or scan the QR Code below:

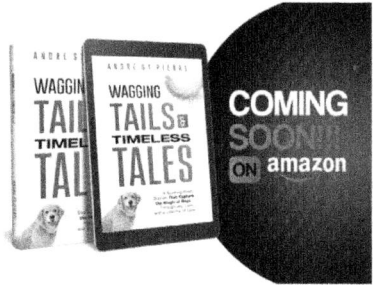

Inside the book of short stories, you will discover:

> 🐾**Nine heartwarming stories**

> 🐾**Tales of unconditional love**

> 🐾**The bittersweet reality of saying goodbye**

> 🐾**How dogs help us heal**

If you want to **laugh, cry and smile** make sure to grab the free book today.

Introduction

Bringing a puppy into your home is an exciting and rewarding experience. They're full of energy, curiosity, and unconditional love. But with all that joy comes responsibility—especially when it comes to training. If you're a busy person or family, the thought of training a puppy might seem overwhelming. After all, you already have a packed schedule—work, errands, family obligations, and everything else life throws at you. So how do you find the time to teach your puppy the essential skills they need to become a well-behaved, happy member of the family?

In this book, we're going to show you that puppy training doesn't have to be complicated or time-consuming. In fact, with just 10 minutes a day, you can create a strong, positive foundation for your puppy that will pay off for years to come. But before we dive into the practical steps, let's explore why puppy training is so important and how you can successfully fit it into your busy life.

The Benefits of a Well-Trained Puppy

A well-trained puppy is more than just a cute and well-behaved companion—it's a foundation for a lifelong bond built on trust, respect, and mutual understanding. When your puppy knows what to expect from you and the world around them, it leads to less stress for both of you. Here's how:

- **Happier, Healthier Relationships**
  Training helps your puppy understand the boundaries and expectations in your home. When they know where it's okay to go, what they can chew, and what behaviors are acceptable, they feel more secure and confident. A puppy that's been taught how to behave around people, pets, and in various environments is less likely to develop anxiety or behavioral issues later on. A well-trained dog is also a pleasure to be around, which makes your relationship stronger and more enjoyable.

- **Better Control and Safety**
  Imagine being able to call your puppy to come back to you on command, even when they're excited or distracted. This kind of control not only makes your walks and outings more

enjoyable, but it also helps keep your puppy safe in situations where they might get too curious, like running into traffic or darting toward another dog. Training your puppy to respond to basic commands can literally be life-saving.

- **A More Peaceful Home**
  Puppies are naturally curious and energetic, which can lead to destructive behaviors if not directed properly. A well-trained puppy won't chew on furniture, jump on guests, or bark uncontrollably. Instead, they'll know how to relax and settle down when it's time to rest. A calm, obedient dog leads to a calm, happy home—and that means less stress for you, too.

What to Expect Along the Way

Training your puppy is a journey, not a race. Expect progress, but also setbacks—and that's okay. Here's what you can anticipate as you move forward:

- **The First Few Weeks: The Learning Curve**
  In the beginning, it's normal for your puppy to seem distracted or confused. Just like any new skill, it takes time for them to get the hang of things. But don't be discouraged. Puppies are

quick learners, and with consistency, they will start to understand the basics of potty training, leash walking, and simple commands like "sit" and "stay." At this stage, patience and repetition are your best friends.

- **Challenges Along the Way**
  As your puppy grows, they'll be exposed to more distractions, new environments, and different situations. This is when challenges might arise—your puppy might start pulling on the leash, barking more, or getting distracted during training sessions. It's important to remember that these are normal parts of the learning process. The key is to remain consistent, calm, and focused on positive reinforcement. Each small success adds up.

- **The Sweet Spot: When Things Click**
  After a few weeks or months of consistent training, you'll notice your puppy starting to respond reliably to commands. They'll start to look to you for guidance, and you'll notice their behavior becoming more predictable and manageable. This is the moment when you'll realize that your 10-minute training sessions are paying off—and that your puppy is becoming

the well-behaved companion you've always wanted. It's also when the bond between you and your puppy deepens, as they begin to trust you more and more.

How to Incorporate Puppy Training into Your Busy Schedule

If you're like most people, you've got a lot on your plate—and finding extra time in your day can seem impossible. But here's the good news: you don't need hours of free time to train your puppy. In fact, a consistent 10-minute training routine is all it takes to make significant progress. Here's how to fit training into your busy schedule:

- **Short, Focused Sessions**
  Puppies have short attention spans, and so do we. That's why 10-minute training sessions work so well. These short bursts of focused attention help your puppy stay engaged and learn without getting overwhelmed. Plus, 10 minutes is easy to fit in—whether it's in the morning before work, during a lunch break, or in the evening while you wind down. Consistency is more important

than duration, so don't worry about setting aside huge chunks of time.

- **Training During Everyday Activities**
  You don't have to stop everything to train your puppy. Training can be integrated into your daily life in simple, effective ways. For example, you can practice commands while you're preparing dinner ("sit" before the food bowl), on your walks ("heel" or "leave it"), or during playtime ("fetch" and "drop it"). The more you weave training into everyday moments, the easier it becomes. It won't feel like an extra task—it'll just be part of your routine.

- **Get the Whole Family Involved**
  If you're juggling multiple family members or housemates, getting everyone on the same page can be a huge help. Make sure everyone in your household uses the same commands and reinforcement techniques to avoid confusing the puppy. Assign different family members small tasks, like feeding, potty breaks, or practicing specific commands. This will help distribute the responsibility of training and make it feel less burdensome.

A Positive, Sustainable Approach to Puppy Training

Training your puppy doesn't have to feel like a chore. With the right mindset and a few simple strategies, you can create a positive, manageable training routine that fits into your life. The goal is not perfection—it's progress. Even with a busy schedule, you can raise a well-behaved, happy puppy with just 10 minutes of training each day. In the chapters ahead, we'll show you exactly how to do this—step-by-step—so you can enjoy the rewards of a well-trained, content puppy without the stress.

By the end of this book, you'll have the tools and strategies to transform your puppy into a well-behaved companion, all while maintaining balance in your busy life. And best of all, you'll have the peace of mind that comes with knowing you're creating a strong foundation for your puppy's future—and for the bond between you. Let's get started!

Chapter 1

Setting the Stage for Success

The Importance of Early Training

Training your puppy during the first few months of their life is one of the most impactful things you can do to ensure they grow into a well-behaved, well-adjusted adult dog. These early months are a critical window for learning, and what your puppy experiences during this time will set the foundation for their behavior and emotional development for years to come. Let's explore why early socialization, starting with small, consistent training sessions, and positive reinforcement are essential for long-term success.

1. Why Early Socialization and Obedience Are Key to a Well-Adjusted Puppy

The foundation of a well-adjusted puppy is built on early socialization and obedience training. These two aspects of early learning are key to ensuring that your puppy grows into a confident, well-behaved dog who can handle new situations, environments, and people with ease.

- **Reducing Fear and Aggression Through Socialization**
  Socialization refers to exposing your puppy to different people, animals, sounds, and environments in a positive and controlled manner. This helps your puppy understand that new experiences aren't something to fear. A well-socialized puppy is more likely to grow into an adult dog who is comfortable in a variety of situations—whether it's meeting new people, walking in busy areas, or being around other dogs. Puppies who miss this critical socialization period can develop fears and phobias, which may turn into aggressive behavior later in life.

- **Building Obedience for Better Control and Safety**
  Basic obedience training teaches your puppy the foundation for good behavior. Commands like "sit," "stay," and "come" are not only essential for day-to-day interactions but also provide you with the ability to control your puppy in various situations. Early obedience training ensures that your puppy learns to listen to you, even when

they're distracted, which can be a lifesaver when you're out in public or need to prevent dangerous behavior.

- **Preventing Behavioral Issues**
  Early obedience training helps prevent common behavioral issues like jumping, barking, chewing, and digging. When you teach your puppy what's expected of them from the start, you create clear boundaries. This reduces the likelihood of unwanted behaviors developing as they get older. The sooner you start, the easier it will be to correct minor issues before they become ingrained habits.

2. How Starting Small, Early Training Sessions Create Long-Term Success

Starting with small, manageable training sessions during your puppy's early months sets the stage for long-term success. Puppies learn best through short bursts of focused activity, and by keeping training sessions brief but consistent, you can ensure that your puppy remains engaged and focused.

- **Maximizing Focus with Short Sessions**
  Puppies, especially in their early stages, have short attention spans. Trying to train for

extended periods can lead to frustration for both you and your puppy. Instead, aim for training sessions that last no more than 5 to 10 minutes at a time. Short sessions help your puppy stay focused and prevent them from getting overwhelmed. By consistently practicing throughout the day, you're reinforcing their learning without risking burnout.

- **Building Gradually for Long-Term Mastery**
  When you start small, you allow your puppy to build a solid foundation of basic skills. Begin with simple commands like "sit" and "stay," and as your puppy masters these, gradually increase the difficulty of the tasks. This step-by-step approach prevents your puppy from feeling overwhelmed and sets them up for success as they learn more complex skills. Over time, the small, consistent steps you take will add up to major behavioral improvements.

- **Establishing a Routine for Success**
  Starting with small training sessions helps establish a regular routine. Puppies thrive on consistency, and creating a predictable pattern of training throughout the day helps them understand that learning is a fun, ongoing

process. This also sets expectations for both you and your puppy, making training feel like a natural part of your daily life rather than a burdensome task.

3. Understanding the Impact of Consistent, Positive Reinforcement on Your Puppy's Behavior

One of the most effective training tools you can use with your puppy is positive reinforcement. This method involves rewarding your puppy for good behavior, helping them understand what behaviors are desirable. The consistency and positivity you use in training have a direct impact on how your puppy responds to learning and how they behave in the long term.

- **Building Positive Associations**
  Positive reinforcement works by creating strong, positive associations in your puppy's mind. When they perform a desired behavior—such as sitting, coming when called, or staying calm during a vet visit—and receive a reward (like a treat, praise, or playtime), they learn to associate that behavior with a positive outcome. Over time, your puppy will start to repeat these behaviors because they've learned that they lead

to something good. This positive association strengthens the desired behavior and makes it more likely to stick.

- **Consistency Reinforces Learning**
  Consistency is key when using positive reinforcement. Puppies learn best when the rewards for good behavior are predictable and reliable. If your puppy sits and gets a treat, but sometimes you withhold the treat without explanation, they may become confused. Clear, consistent rewards help your puppy understand exactly what behavior you're rewarding, and they'll be more motivated to repeat that behavior in the future.

- **Fostering a Willingness to Learn**
  Consistent, positive reinforcement creates an environment where your puppy feels motivated and eager to learn. Puppies who are rewarded for good behavior are more likely to engage in training sessions and look to you for guidance. When training is fun and rewarding, your puppy will enjoy learning new skills, making the entire process easier and more enjoyable for both of you.

Conclusion

Early training is the key to raising a well-behaved, confident, and well-adjusted puppy. By focusing on early socialization and obedience, starting with small, manageable training sessions, and using consistent positive reinforcement, you're setting your puppy up for success both now and in the future. The skills and behaviors they learn in their early months will influence their behavior for the rest of their lives, and the time you invest in training now will pay off in the form of a happy, well-behaved dog who is a joy to be around.

The Power of Consistency

When it comes to puppy training, consistency is the key to success. Puppies, like all dogs, thrive on predictability. When training is consistent—across commands, timing, and rewards—it creates a stable framework for your puppy to learn and understand what is expected of them. Whether you're teaching basic commands or addressing behavioral issues, consistency helps your puppy feel secure and supported, which in turn makes learning easier and more effective.

In this section, we'll explore why consistency is so important and how you can integrate it seamlessly into your daily routine to ensure lasting success with your puppy.

1. Why Consistency in Commands, Timing, and Rewards is Essential

Consistency in training means your puppy always knows what to expect from you. When you maintain consistent commands, timing, and rewards, you make the learning process clearer and more straightforward for your puppy. Here's why each of these elements is so important:

- **Clear Commands and Expectations**
  Using the same word for the same command each time helps your puppy learn faster. For example, if you say "sit" one time and "down" the next time for the same behavior, your puppy will become confused. Pick simple, distinct words for commands and stick with them. The clarity in your communication helps your puppy connect the word to the action, reducing frustration for both of you.

- **Timely Reinforcement is Crucial**
  Puppies live in the moment. The more immediate the reward, the clearer the connection between their behavior and the outcome. If you reward your puppy too late,

they may not understand why they're being rewarded. For instance, if your puppy sits and you wait 30 seconds to give them a treat, they may associate the reward with something that happened earlier and not the sitting behavior itself. Aim to reward right after the desired behavior, within a few seconds, so your puppy knows exactly what they're being praised for.

- **Reinforcing Positive Behavior Consistently** Positive reinforcement is most effective when it is consistent. If your puppy sits for a treat one time and is ignored the next time, they may lose motivation to repeat the behavior. The consistency of rewards, whether it's a treat, praise, or play, reinforces the idea that the desired behavior leads to a positive outcome. This builds a strong habit that your puppy will continue to follow.

2. How to Create Simple Routines That Integrate Training into Your Everyday Life

The beauty of consistency is that it doesn't have to mean long, rigid training sessions. You can easily integrate training into your everyday life by creating simple, repetitive routines. This makes training feel less like a chore and more like a natural part of your day. Here are a few ways to do this:

- **Incorporate Training into Daily Activities**
  Training doesn't need to be a separate task. You can use everyday activities as training opportunities. For example, before you feed your puppy, ask them to "sit" and wait calmly before you place the bowl down. During walks, reinforce leash walking by rewarding them when they walk nicely by your side. Every interaction with your puppy can be a chance to practice basic commands like "sit," "stay," "come," and "down." These small moments add up and make training feel more like an organic part of your routine rather than a separate activity.

- **Create Consistent Rituals**
  Whether it's potty training, crate training, or bedtime routines, having a set structure helps your puppy learn the rhythm of daily life. For example, you might always take your puppy outside for a potty break first thing in the morning, after meals, and before bedtime. Consistent routines help your puppy understand what's expected and when, making them feel more secure and less anxious.

- **Short and Frequent Sessions**

  Puppies have short attention spans, so rather than dedicating long periods to training, break it into shorter, more frequent sessions. This keeps your puppy engaged and prevents them from getting overwhelmed or bored. Just 5-10 minutes of training several times a day can make a huge difference in your puppy's ability to learn and retain new skills. You can easily integrate these mini-sessions throughout the day—before meals, after playtime, or during a quiet moment in the afternoon.

3. The Importance of Everyone in the Household Being on the Same Page

If you live in a household with multiple people, it's important that everyone is on the same page when it comes to training your puppy. Inconsistent rules or commands can confuse your puppy and slow their learning progress. By ensuring that all household members are using the same commands, rewards, and routines, you create a unified, predictable environment that your puppy can easily understand.

- **Unified Commands and Rules**

  Everyone in the household should use the same

word for each command. For example, if one person uses "sit" and another uses "down" for the same action, your puppy won't understand which command to follow. Agree on a set of commands that everyone will use consistently. This consistency in language makes training clearer for your puppy, and it also makes the process smoother for you.

- **Consistency in Rewards**

  Everyone should also be on the same page about what constitutes a reward. If one person gives a treat for sitting and another just offers praise, your puppy might get confused about which behavior is worth repeating. Make sure that all family members are on the same page about when and how to reward your puppy for good behavior.

- **Shared Responsibility for Training**

  Training a puppy is a team effort, and it's easier when everyone in the household participates. Whether it's feeding, potty training, or reinforcing good behavior, having all members of the household involved makes it more likely that your puppy will learn quickly and consistently. Everyone should know what the puppy is being trained to do, and everyone should reinforce those behaviors consistently.

Conclusion

Consistency is one of the most powerful tools in your puppy training toolkit. By maintaining consistent commands, timing, and rewards, you make it easier for your puppy to understand what's expected and how to meet those expectations. Integrating training into your daily routine keeps it manageable and natural, while ensuring that everyone in the household is on the same page guarantees that your puppy receives clear and predictable guidance. With consistency, training becomes less of a task and more of an enjoyable, ongoing part of your life with your puppy. This consistency will pay off in the form of a well-behaved, confident dog who is happy to follow your lead.

Setting Realistic Goals

Training a puppy doesn't need to be a time-consuming, stressful task. With just 10 minutes of focused training a day, you can achieve meaningful progress that sets the stage for a well-behaved, happy dog. By setting realistic goals, focusing on key behaviors, and breaking the training process into manageable steps, you'll make consistent, long-term progress without feeling overwhelmed. Let's explore how to set achievable goals that work with your busy schedule while helping your puppy thrive.

1. What You Can Realistically Achieve with Just 10 Minutes of Training a Day

It's easy to feel like training a puppy requires hours of dedicated time, but the reality is that you can make significant strides with just a few minutes of focused training each day. With consistency and intention, short training sessions can be highly effective, especially when integrated into your daily routine.

- **Learning Basic Commands**
  In just 10 minutes a day, you can teach your puppy essential commands like "sit," "stay," "come," and "down." Short, focused training sessions help your puppy stay engaged and retain new information more effectively. By breaking down the training into small, digestible parts, you create a clear learning environment that makes it easier for your puppy to grasp these foundational skills.

- **Building Focus and Impulse Control**
  Even in just 10 minutes, you can work on

building your puppy's attention span and impulse control. For example, practicing "leave it" or "wait" during meal times, or teaching them to stay calmly in their crate, can be accomplished in brief sessions. The goal is to gradually increase your puppy's ability to focus on you and remain calm in various situations, which will pay off in the long run.

- **Reinforcing Good Behavior Throughout the Day**
  It's not just the structured training sessions that count—it's also about reinforcing good behavior throughout the day. Use small, everyday moments to reward good behavior, such as praising your puppy when they follow a command or behave calmly in a new situation. These short bursts of positive reinforcement can be just as powerful as formal training sessions and help your puppy understand what's expected.

2. Identifying the Core Behaviors to Focus on in the Early Stages of Training

When starting with a new puppy, it's important not to overwhelm yourself by trying to teach everything at once.

Instead, focus on the core behaviors that will lay the foundation for good habits and help your puppy succeed in the long term. Here are the most essential skills to prioritize in the early stages of training:

- **Housebreaking and Potty Training**
  One of the first things you'll need to address is potty training. Teaching your puppy where and when to go potty is critical to preventing accidents around the house. Early consistency in taking your puppy outside at regular intervals (first thing in the morning, after meals, before bed) will help them learn where it's appropriate to relieve themselves. Potty training should be your priority in the first few weeks, as it provides the structure your puppy needs to feel comfortable in their new home.

- **Basic Commands: Sit, Stay, Come**
  Teaching your puppy to respond to basic commands is key to creating a well-behaved dog. "Sit" is usually the easiest command to start with, as it helps to build your puppy's focus and self-control. Once your puppy masters "sit," move on to "stay" and "come"—two commands that are essential for your puppy's safety and your peace of mind. For example, "stay" helps

prevent jumping on guests or running into dangerous situations, while "come" ensures your puppy returns to you when called, even if they're distracted.

- **Leash Walking and Crate Training**
  Leash walking and crate training are two practical skills that make your daily life with your puppy much easier. Early leash training teaches your puppy not to pull or dart in different directions, while crate training helps with housebreaking and provides your puppy with a safe, secure space. Both of these skills also promote good behavior when you're out and about, making public outings and car trips less stressful.

3. Setting Short-Term Goals for Your Puppy's Growth and Long-Term Success

Setting goals is an essential part of the training process. By setting both short-term and long-term goals, you can measure your puppy's progress and stay motivated. It's important to be flexible with your goals, adjusting them as needed to fit your puppy's development and temperament.

- **Short-Term Goals: Building Foundational Skills**

  Short-term goals are focused on building the basics and should be achievable within a few days or weeks. Examples of short-term goals include:

  - Teaching your puppy to sit on command within a week.

  - Having your puppy learn to stay in one spot for 30 seconds by the end of the second week.

  - Successfully walking on a leash without pulling during daily walks within 1-2 weeks.

- These goals are small but impactful, and they help build the foundation for more advanced training in the future. Short-term goals keep you focused on what's immediately important while creating momentum for continued success.

- **Medium-Term Goals: Strengthening and Expanding Skills**

  Once your puppy has mastered the basics, you can set medium-term goals. These are goals that take a little more time but are essential for your puppy's development. Examples include:

- ○ Increasing the duration of "stay" to a minute or more.

- ○ Successfully walking on a leash without distractions, such as other dogs or people, within a month.

- ○ Mastering basic commands even when there are distractions, like in the park or around guests.

- These goals help refine your puppy's behavior and improve their ability to respond to commands in more challenging environments.

- **Long-Term Goals: Well-Behaved and Confident Adult Dog**
  Long-term goals should focus on your puppy's overall behavior as they mature into adulthood. These goals might take several months to achieve and include things like:

  - ○ Having your puppy consistently follow commands in a variety of environments, from the park to the beach.

- Ensuring your puppy is calm and well-behaved in public settings, such as on walks, at the vet, or in social gatherings.

- Maintaining positive behavior habits for life, like crate training, leash walking, and appropriate potty habits.

- Long-term goals are about fostering a balanced, well-adjusted adult dog. These goals should be viewed as ongoing, not something to be "finished" but continually developed throughout your dog's life.

Conclusion

Setting realistic, achievable goals for your puppy's training is an essential part of the process. With just 10 minutes of focused training a day, you can teach foundational behaviors, reinforce good habits, and make steady progress toward your long-term success. By focusing on the core behaviors—such as housebreaking, basic commands, and leash training—and setting short-term goals that build on each other, you'll set your puppy up for growth and confidence. With patience and consistency, you'll watch your puppy grow from a curious bundle of energy into a well-behaved, happy adult dog.

Creating a Puppy-Friendly Environment

One of the most important aspects of puppy training is setting up an environment that promotes positive behaviors and discourages unwanted ones. Puppies are naturally curious, and their environment plays a crucial role in their development. By puppy-proofing your home, establishing safe spaces, and using tools like gates and playpens, you can create an environment that encourages learning, reduces accidents, and makes training more effective. Let's take a closer look at how to make your home a puppy-friendly space.

1. Puppy-Proofing Your Space to Prevent Unwanted Behaviors

Puppy-proofing is about setting up your home in a way that minimizes opportunities for your puppy to engage in unwanted or dangerous behaviors. By creating a safe, stimulating environment, you help your puppy learn what is and isn't acceptable, making training easier and more successful.

- **Removing Temptations and Hazards**
  Puppies tend to chew on anything they can get their teeth on—shoes, furniture, cords, and even household plants. Take a look around your

home and identify items that could become potential chew toys or safety hazards. Use cord protectors to cover electrical cables, move shoes or other tempting items out of reach, and remove toxic plants from your puppy's environment. The less opportunity there is for your puppy to chew on inappropriate items, the fewer chances they'll have to develop bad habits.

- **Designating Puppy-Friendly Zones**
  It's a good idea to set up a designated space for your puppy where they can explore, play, and learn without causing damage to your home. This could be a specific room or an area with puppy-friendly items—like toys, a comfortable bed, and safe chew items. Keeping your puppy confined to this area when you're not actively supervising them can help prevent accidents and unwanted behaviors like chewing on furniture or getting into trash cans.

- **Using Puppy-Proofing as a Learning Tool**
  Puppy-proofing can also serve as an opportunity for training. For example, you can set up designated areas with "no-go" zones that your puppy is not allowed to enter. Using baby gates or crates to section off rooms can teach your

puppy boundaries, helping them learn where it's safe to roam and where they need to stay out. As your puppy matures and becomes more reliable, you can slowly expand their access to different areas of the house.

2. Establishing a Safe Area for Training and Downtime

A safe area, or designated "training zone," is a space where your puppy can focus on learning, practice commands, or just relax and unwind. This helps separate playtime from work time and provides a calm, secure environment where your puppy can rest or cool down after training sessions.

- **Choosing the Right Spot for Training**
  Select a quiet, distraction-free area for your training sessions. It doesn't need to be large—just enough space for your puppy to focus on you and practice basic commands. A safe area for training could be in your living room, a hallway, or even in your backyard, as long as distractions like other pets, children, or loud noises are minimized. The idea is to create a calm space where your puppy can stay engaged and focused during short training sessions.

- **Creating a Cozy, Comfortable Resting Spot**
  Puppies need a lot of rest to grow and recharge,
  so providing a comfortable and secure space for
  them to relax is essential. This could be a crate, a
  soft bed, or a blanket in a quiet area of your
  home where they can unwind without
  interruption. Having a consistent place to rest
  also helps your puppy learn to settle down and
  helps them understand when it's time to be calm
  and take a break. If your puppy has a designated
  "downtime area," they're less likely to get into
  trouble when left alone.

- **Using Crates for Safety and Structure**
  Crates are a wonderful tool for creating a safe
  and secure space for your puppy. A crate can
  provide a place for them to sleep, relax, or retreat
  when they need some quiet time. It can also help
  with housebreaking and prevent your puppy
  from getting into trouble when you're not home
  or when you're busy. Make sure the crate is not
  used as punishment, but rather as a cozy den-like
  space that your puppy associates with positive
  experiences. You can also use the crate for brief
  training sessions to help your puppy build
  positive associations with being contained.

3. Using Gates or Playpens to Set Boundaries and Encourage Safe Exploration

While puppies need freedom to explore, it's important to establish clear boundaries that keep them safe and prevent them from getting into mischief. Baby gates and playpens are great tools for managing where your puppy can go and allowing them to explore safely in a controlled environment.

- **Setting Boundaries with Baby Gates**
  Baby gates are a simple and effective way to section off areas of your home and prevent your puppy from roaming into rooms where they might get into trouble. Whether it's the kitchen, the bathroom, or a bedroom with valuables, gates allow you to keep your puppy safe and prevent unwanted behaviors like eating non-food items or getting into harmful situations. Gates can also be used to separate areas where your puppy can play or train from areas where they should not go, like a home office or dining area.

- **Using Playpens for Controlled Exploration**
  A playpen or puppy pen creates a contained space where your puppy can explore safely

without getting into trouble. Playpens can be used indoors or outdoors to give your puppy room to move around, play with toys, and engage in positive behaviors while you supervise from a distance. Playpens are especially useful for puppies that are still learning to regulate their impulses or for those who tend to chew on things they shouldn't. It gives your puppy a safe place to burn off energy without the risk of damaging your home or getting into hazardous areas.

- **Promoting Safe Exploration and Independence**

  By using gates or playpens to restrict your puppy's access to certain areas, you're teaching them boundaries while still allowing them to explore and engage with their environment. Gradually increase their freedom as they learn to follow commands and demonstrate good behavior. Over time, you can remove the gates or playpens in certain areas, giving your puppy more freedom to explore your home, but only after they've proven they can be trusted to make good choices.

Conclusion

Creating a puppy-friendly environment is an essential part of the training process. By puppy-proofing your home, setting up a safe area for training and rest, and using tools like gates and playpens to manage your puppy's environment, you can set them up for success. This not only helps to prevent unwanted behaviors but also allows your puppy to safely explore, learn, and grow in a controlled space. A well-designed environment encourages positive behaviors, supports effective training, and promotes a calm, happy atmosphere where both you and your puppy can thrive.

Setting Up a Training Routine

A successful puppy training routine doesn't require hours of dedicated time—what matters most is consistency, structure, and incorporating training into your daily life. By creating a schedule that includes regular feeding, potty breaks, and brief training sessions, you can make progress with your puppy even with a busy lifestyle. The goal is to establish a rhythm that works for both you and your puppy, ensuring that training becomes a seamless part of your day. Let's dive into how you can set up a realistic and effective training routine that fits into your schedule.

1. Creating a Daily Schedule That Includes Consistent Feeding, Potty Breaks, and Training

Establishing a clear, predictable daily schedule is one of the most effective ways to ensure your puppy learns the structure and routine they need to thrive. Consistency in feeding, potty breaks, and training times helps your puppy feel secure and know what to expect throughout the day.

- **Set Regular Feeding Times**

  Feeding your puppy at consistent times each day helps regulate their digestive system and makes it easier to plan potty breaks. Puppies generally need to eat three times a day, and having a set feeding schedule makes housebreaking easier because you'll know when your puppy is likely to need a bathroom break afterward. For example, if you feed your puppy at 7 a.m., 12 p.m., and 5 p.m., you can plan potty breaks shortly after each meal.

- **Plan Potty Breaks and Outdoor Time**

  Potty training is one of the most important aspects of early puppy training, and setting a routine for potty breaks is essential. Puppies generally need to go outside to relieve themselves within 15-30 minutes of eating, drinking, or waking up from a nap. By setting a schedule that includes regular potty breaks, you can prevent accidents and help your puppy learn where it's appropriate to go. For example, you might take your puppy outside after every meal and nap, as well as before and after training sessions.

- **Build in Training Sessions**
  Training doesn't need to take a lot of time— short, focused sessions of 5-10 minutes are perfect for puppies. Include these brief training sessions in your daily schedule, ideally after a potty break and before your puppy becomes too tired or distracted. Early morning or late evening are good times for training, as your puppy is likely to be more focused and receptive. For example, after breakfast and a quick potty break, you can spend 5 minutes practicing basic commands like "sit" or "stay" before your puppy's energy levels dip.

2. How to Incorporate Training into Everyday Activities (e.g., Mealtime, Walks)

Training doesn't always have to happen in a designated training session—it can be woven into your daily activities. By taking advantage of natural opportunities throughout the day, you can reinforce good behavior and help your puppy learn essential skills while you're carrying on with your regular routine.

- **Training During Mealtimes**
  Mealtime is a perfect opportunity to reinforce basic commands like "sit" and "stay." Before you serve your puppy's food, ask them to "sit" and wait for a few seconds before you place the bowl down. This not only teaches patience but also reinforces the "stay" command. You can also practice self-control during mealtimes by requiring your puppy to wait for permission (e.g., a verbal cue like "okay" or "go ahead") before they start eating.

- **Incorporating Training During Walks**
  Walks are a great opportunity to work on leash manners and recall training. Every time you go out for a walk, you can practice basic commands like "sit," "heel," and "leave it" in a real-world setting. For example, when you stop to cross the street, you can have your puppy sit and stay until you give the release command. If your puppy starts pulling on the leash, use "heel" to encourage them to walk calmly by your side.

Walks also provide an opportunity to practice recall by calling your puppy to you and rewarding them when they return.

- **Using Playtime as a Training Opportunity**
  Playtime can also be a training opportunity. During fetch or tug-of-war, you can incorporate commands like "drop it," "sit," and "stay." Play is a natural way to keep your puppy engaged, and by adding a few commands during playtime, you reinforce training while making it fun. For example, before throwing the ball, ask your puppy to sit and wait. You can also use playtime to work on impulse control by teaching them to wait for your signal before chasing the toy.

3. Recognizing Natural Windows for Training in Your Busy Schedule (e.g., Mornings, During TV Time)

One of the best parts of puppy training is that you don't need to carve out hours of time each day to see progress. By recognizing natural "windows" in your day when your puppy is most receptive to training, you can make the most of your limited time. Here are a few opportunities that may naturally fit into your schedule:

- **Morning Time: The Best Time for Focused Training**
  Puppies tend to be most alert and focused in the mornings after a good night's rest. If possible, schedule a brief training session right after your puppy wakes up and before they've had breakfast. This is often the best time to practice commands or reinforce behaviors because your puppy is rested, ready to learn, and more likely to focus on you.

- **TV or Relaxing Time: Training During Calm Moments**
  You can use quiet, relaxing moments, like when you're watching TV or winding down at the end of the day, as an opportunity for low-key training. During these times, you can work on things like impulse control, staying calm, or practicing "settle" commands. For example, while you're sitting on the couch, ask your puppy to "sit" or "stay" for a few seconds before rewarding them. This not only reinforces commands but helps your puppy learn to be calm and relaxed during quieter moments.

- **Potty Breaks as Training Opportunities**
  Potty breaks are a natural part of your day, and

you can use them as mini training sessions. For example, after your puppy does their business, you can ask for a "sit" or "stay" before heading back inside. Potty breaks also give you a chance to work on leash manners and socialization, as you can introduce your puppy to new environments, people, or other dogs while reinforcing good behavior.

Conclusion

Creating a training routine that fits into your busy schedule is all about making the most of the time you already have. By setting a consistent schedule for feeding, potty breaks, and training sessions, and by integrating training into everyday activities like walks and mealtimes, you can ensure that your puppy is learning and progressing each day. Recognizing natural windows for training, whether it's during morning time, TV time, or potty breaks, allows you to use your day more efficiently. With a little planning and consistency, you'll be able to train your puppy effectively—even with a hectic schedule. The key is to make training feel like a natural part of your day, rather than a task that adds extra stress.

Crate Training Basics

Crate training is one of the most valuable tools in a puppy owner's toolkit. Not only does it help with housebreaking and preventing accidents, but it also provides your puppy with a safe and secure space to rest, relax, and feel comfortable when you're not around. Done correctly, crate training can establish routines, promote good behavior, and give your puppy a sense of structure in their new home. Let's dive into the basics of crate training and how to make the experience positive for both you and your puppy.

1. The Benefits of Crate Training for Housebreaking and as a Safe Space

Crate training offers multiple benefits, both for housebreaking and for providing your puppy with a secure, personal space where they can feel safe and calm.

- **Effective Housebreaking Tool**
  A crate is one of the most effective tools for housebreaking a puppy. Dogs instinctively avoid soiling their sleeping area, so a properly-sized crate can help teach your puppy to hold their bladder until they are let outside. When used consistently, a crate will help establish a routine

for potty breaks, which is crucial for housebreaking. By crating your puppy when you're not able to supervise them directly, you reduce the chances of accidents in the house and reinforce the habit of going outside to relieve themselves.

- **A Safe, Secure Space**
  Beyond housebreaking, a crate provides your puppy with a safe space to rest and retreat to when they need some quiet time. This can be especially important for a new puppy adjusting to their new home. The crate becomes their personal den—a place where they can feel secure and comfortable. Whether you're at home or away, a crate offers your puppy a cozy, protected area where they won't get into trouble or feel overwhelmed by too much activity. A crate can also serve as a training tool for teaching boundaries and separation from you when needed.

- **Prevents Destructive Behavior**
  When left unsupervised, puppies can quickly get into trouble by chewing on furniture, electrical cords, or other household items. Crating your puppy when you're away or unable to supervise

them ensures they're not engaging in destructive behaviors, and it protects your home from potential damage. Crates are a safe place where your puppy can't access dangerous objects or get into things they shouldn't, like trash or food left out.

2. Making the Crate a Positive Place with Treats and Short Sessions

The key to successful crate training is making the crate a positive, inviting place for your puppy. If your puppy associates the crate with good things, they'll be more likely to view it as a safe, comfortable space instead of a form of punishment.

- **Introduce the Crate Gradually**
  Start by introducing the crate to your puppy in a calm, positive way. Leave the crate door open at first and let your puppy explore it on their own. Place some of your puppy's favorite toys or a soft blanket inside to make it more inviting. Encourage them to go in and out at their own pace, without forcing them. Let them sniff around and get comfortable with the crate at their own speed.

- **Use Treats to Create Positive Associations**
One of the best ways to help your puppy form positive associations with the crate is by using treats. Put a few treats inside the crate or place them just beyond the crate's entrance so that your puppy has to go inside to get them. Over time, they'll begin to associate the crate with something positive—whether it's a treat, a meal, or a fun toy. You can also use treats during training sessions to reinforce the idea that the crate is a safe, pleasant space.

- **Short, Positive Sessions**
When you first start crate training, keep the sessions short to avoid overwhelming your puppy. Start by placing your puppy in the crate for just a few minutes at a time while you're nearby. Gradually increase the length of time as your puppy becomes more comfortable with being inside. During these short sessions, offer praise and rewards for calm behavior. Never force your puppy into the crate or use it as a form of punishment, as this can create negative associations that make crate training more difficult.

3. Ensuring Your Puppy's Crate Experience is Comfortable and Calm

A well-set-up, comfortable crate environment will help your puppy feel relaxed and secure. The goal is for the crate to be a place of comfort and relaxation, not stress or anxiety. Let's take a look at how to make the crate experience as comfortable and calm as possible for your puppy.

- **Choose the Right Size Crate**
  The size of the crate is important for both safety and comfort. The crate should be large enough for your puppy to stand up, turn around, and lie down comfortably, but not so large that they can use one corner as a bathroom area. If the crate is too large, your puppy might not feel the need to hold their bladder, and accidents can happen. A crate that's the right size will encourage your puppy to settle in and make the space feel secure and cozy.

- **Create a Comfortable Interior**
  Make the crate as inviting as possible by adding soft bedding, a blanket, or a pillow inside. Puppies often feel more at ease when they have something soft to rest on. You can also place a

favorite toy or chew item in the crate to give your puppy something to focus on. If your puppy enjoys comfort, you could also add an item with your scent, like a piece of your clothing, to make the space feel more familiar and reassuring.

- **Keep the Crate in a Calm Location**

  The location of the crate can make a big difference in your puppy's experience. Place the crate in a quiet area of your home where your puppy won't be constantly disturbed by noise or distractions. Avoid putting the crate in high-traffic areas or near loud appliances. However, it's also important not to isolate your puppy too much. Keep the crate in a place where they can still see and hear you when you're home, as this will help reduce any feelings of loneliness or anxiety.

Conclusion

Crate training is an essential part of raising a well-behaved and well-adjusted puppy. By using the crate as both a housebreaking tool and a safe retreat, you can help your puppy develop a sense of structure and security in their new home. The key to successful crate training is making the experience positive, comfortable, and calm. Gradually introducing your puppy to the crate, using treats to build positive associations, and ensuring the crate is a comfortable space will set the stage for a successful training process. With time and patience, your puppy will come to see the crate as a cozy, secure space they can enjoy, and it will become an important part of their daily routine.

Investing in the Right Training Equipment

Training a puppy doesn't just rely on your time and patience; having the right tools can make a significant difference in your success. The right training equipment helps reinforce good behaviors, creates a structured training environment, and ensures that your puppy remains engaged and motivated throughout the process. In this section, we'll discuss the essential tools every puppy owner should have, how to use them effectively, and why investing in the right equipment makes all the difference.

1. Essential Tools: Clicker, Treats, Leash, Collar, and Puppy-Friendly Toys

When it comes to puppy training, having the right tools can make training sessions more efficient and enjoyable for both you and your puppy. Here's a rundown of the essential training equipment:

- **Clicker**
  A clicker is a small, handheld device that makes a distinct "click" sound when pressed. It's a powerful tool for reinforcing positive behaviors in a precise and consistent manner. The sound of the click marks the exact moment your puppy performs the desired behavior, making it easier for them to understand what they did right. When paired with treats or rewards, a clicker helps create clear, immediate feedback, making learning faster and more effective.

- **Treats**
  Treats are one of the most powerful motivators for puppies during training. Use small, soft treats that are easy for your puppy to eat quickly and don't require chewing. Keep them on hand during training sessions to reward your puppy immediately after they perform the desired

behavior. You can also use treats as a form of positive reinforcement in other situations—like rewarding your puppy after potty breaks or when they settle down in their crate. Make sure to vary the type of treats you use to keep your puppy engaged and motivated.

- **Leash and Collar**
  A leash and collar are essential for walking and controlling your puppy during training. The leash helps you guide your puppy during walks and training sessions, teaching them proper leash manners and helping with recall training. A comfortable collar ensures your puppy is safe while you're out and about. When choosing a collar, ensure it fits snugly but comfortably, allowing room for two fingers to slide underneath. Avoid collars that are too tight or too loose. For training purposes, you can also invest in a harness that discourages pulling and gives you more control over your puppy's movements.

- **Puppy-Friendly Toys**
  Puppy-friendly toys are a must for both training and play. Toys help keep your puppy engaged, reduce boredom, and provide a safe outlet for

their chewing instincts. You'll want a variety of toys for different purposes—chew toys for teething, interactive toys for mental stimulation, and fetch toys for physical exercise. Look for toys that are durable, non-toxic, and the right size for your puppy. Rotating toys regularly helps keep your puppy's interest high, and using toys during training sessions can be a fun way to encourage good behavior.

2. How to Use a Clicker to Reinforce Positive Behaviors

The clicker is a simple yet highly effective tool for reinforcing positive behaviors during puppy training. By associating the sound of the clicker with a reward (usually a treat), you can quickly communicate to your puppy that they've done something right. Here's how to use a clicker effectively:

- **The Basics of Clicker Training**
  The key to using a clicker is consistency. Start by introducing your puppy to the sound of the clicker in a neutral, calm setting. Simply click the device and immediately give your puppy a treat. This helps your puppy form an association between the sound of the clicker and the reward

they receive. After a few repetitions, your puppy will start to understand that the click means a reward is coming, and they'll begin to focus on the behavior that precedes it.

- **Marking the Desired Behavior**
The clicker allows you to mark the exact moment your puppy performs the desired behavior. For example, if you're teaching your puppy to sit, wait for them to lower their rear end to the ground, then immediately click and reward them with a treat. This precise timing helps your puppy understand exactly what action earned the reward, which accelerates the learning process. If you're training for more complex behaviors, like "stay" or "come," use the clicker to mark each step of the behavior as your puppy progresses.

- **Gradually Fading the Clicker**
While the clicker is an effective tool for teaching new behaviors, you eventually want to fade its use and rely more on verbal cues or other forms of reinforcement. After your puppy has learned the behavior and consistently performs it, you can reduce the frequency of clicking and reward with treats or praise instead. The goal is for your

puppy to respond to verbal cues and for the behavior to become ingrained, even without the sound of the clicker.

3. Choosing the Right Toys to Keep Your Puppy Engaged and Stimulated

Toys play a significant role in your puppy's training and overall development. They keep your puppy mentally and physically stimulated, help prevent destructive behavior, and are great for reinforcing positive habits. Here's how to choose and use toys that support both training and play:

- **Chew Toys for Teething and Oral Health**
  Puppies go through a teething phase, which can lead to an increase in chewing behaviors. Providing appropriate chew toys will keep your puppy's teeth and gums healthy and prevent them from chewing on furniture or other household items. Look for toys that are designed specifically for puppies, with materials that are safe for their developing teeth. Rubber or silicone toys are often good choices, as they're soft enough for puppies to chew on but durable enough to withstand their growing teeth.

- **Interactive Toys for Mental Stimulation**
  Puppies are incredibly curious and benefit from toys that challenge their minds. Puzzle toys or treat-dispensing toys are great for keeping your puppy mentally engaged and preventing boredom. These toys often require your puppy to solve a puzzle or figure out how to get a treat out of the toy, which provides both stimulation and entertainment. Interactive toys also serve as a reward for positive behavior, and they can be used in training sessions to keep your puppy focused.

- **Toys for Play and Bonding**
  Play is an important part of puppy development, and having toys for playtime helps strengthen the bond between you and your puppy. Toys like balls, rope toys, or tug-of-war toys are perfect for active play. Incorporating toys into training sessions can also be a fun way to motivate your puppy to perform commands. For example, after your puppy successfully performs a trick or command, you can reward them by playing with their favorite toy. Just be sure to choose toys that are the right size and are safe for your puppy's age and chewing habits.

Conclusion

Investing in the right training equipment is an essential step toward successful puppy training. Tools like a clicker, treats, a leash, a comfortable collar, and puppy-friendly toys not only help in teaching your puppy basic commands and behaviors but also keep them engaged, motivated, and stimulated. The key is to use these tools consistently and effectively, reinforcing positive behaviors and ensuring your puppy enjoys the process. With the right training equipment, you'll be well on your way to raising a well-behaved, happy puppy who is eager to learn and grow.

Using Technology to Your Advantage

In today's digital age, technology can be a valuable tool in the puppy training process. Whether it's tracking your puppy's progress, getting expert advice, or reinforcing commands with audio cues, there are plenty of ways technology can enhance your training experience. The convenience and accessibility of online resources, apps, and virtual training make it easier than ever to fit puppy training into your busy schedule. In this section, we'll explore how to leverage technology to support your puppy's learning, track their progress, and provide personalized guidance.

1. Apps, Videos, and Online Resources for Quick Tips and Tracking Progress

There's an abundance of digital tools available to puppy owners that make training more efficient, interactive, and fun. With just a smartphone, tablet, or computer, you can access a wide range of training materials that guide you through the process, track your puppy's progress, and provide inspiration for new training techniques.

- **Training Apps for Tracking and Progress**
  There are several apps designed specifically for dog training that allow you to track your puppy's progress, set goals, and access quick training tips. Apps like *Puppr*, *Dogo*, or *Zak George's Dog Training* offer step-by-step training programs, complete with videos, challenges, and the ability to track your puppy's success over time. These apps also allow you to record milestones, create a schedule for training sessions, and set reminders to stay on track. Many apps also offer virtual rewards, which can keep both you and your puppy motivated throughout the process.

- **Training Videos for Visual Learning**
  Sometimes it's easier to understand training

techniques by watching them in action. YouTube, Instagram, and dedicated training platforms offer countless videos with demonstrations of everything from basic commands to advanced tricks. Channels like *Zak George's Dog Training Revolution* or *Kikopup* provide clear, easy-to-follow tutorials on a wide range of puppy training topics. Visual learning helps you see how techniques should be executed and gives you confidence in your own ability to train. Additionally, many trainers provide advice on how to handle specific behavior issues, which can be extremely helpful as your puppy progresses.

- **Online Articles, Blogs, and Forums for Support and Ideas**
  If you ever find yourself stuck or needing new ideas, there are endless blogs, forums, and online communities dedicated to puppy training. Websites like *The Spruce Pets*, *American Kennel Club*, or *Cesar's Way* offer articles, expert advice, and practical tips on common training challenges. Dog training forums, such as those found on Reddit or Facebook groups, also provide an opportunity to ask questions, share

your experiences, and get advice from other dog owners. These resources can serve as a valuable support system, especially when you need a quick tip or are troubleshooting an issue with your puppy.

2. How to Make Use of Virtual Dog Training Classes for Personalized Guidance

Sometimes, you need a bit of personalized guidance to ensure that your puppy's training is on the right track. Virtual dog training classes offer flexibility and expert advice from the comfort of your own home. These classes are a great way to get individualized support while still working within your busy schedule.

- **Live Virtual Training Sessions**
  Many trainers now offer live virtual classes that allow you to attend from anywhere. These sessions often include real-time feedback and allow you to interact directly with a trainer. Live virtual sessions can be especially useful if you have specific concerns or need help with a particular aspect of training (e.g., potty training, socialization, or leash manners). Trainers can give you personalized advice and adjust their recommendations based on your puppy's

specific needs. This is a great option for people who want the guidance of a professional but don't have the time to attend in-person classes.

- **Recorded Virtual Classes for Flexibility**
  If your schedule is particularly hectic, recorded virtual dog training classes can be an excellent solution. Many online platforms offer pre-recorded classes that you can watch at your convenience. These classes are typically broken down into modules, making it easy to learn at your own pace. Some platforms also allow you to submit videos of your puppy's progress, so the trainer can provide feedback and adjustments based on your puppy's behavior. Websites like *Dog Trainer Academy*, *Petco*, and *Fenzi Dog Sports Academy* offer flexible online learning options that cover everything from basic obedience to more specialized skills.

- **One-on-One Virtual Consultations**
  If you need more hands-on assistance, many trainers offer one-on-one virtual consultations, where you can video chat with a professional and get personalized, real-time feedback on your puppy's training. This can be particularly helpful if you're working through behavioral

challenges like separation anxiety, excessive barking, or leash reactivity. With a virtual consultation, you can demonstrate how you're currently training, and the trainer can give you specific instructions and tips on how to improve your approach. Personalized advice from an experienced trainer can save you time and effort by addressing issues directly rather than relying solely on generic advice.

3. Incorporating Audio Cues (Like Verbal Commands) and Remote Training Devices

Incorporating technology into your training sessions doesn't have to mean using devices that are overly complex or hard to manage. Simple audio cues and remote training tools can be incredibly effective in reinforcing behaviors, especially when combined with other training methods.

- **Verbal Cues and Audio Commands**
  One of the simplest and most effective ways to train your puppy is through verbal commands. As your puppy learns behaviors, you can pair each behavior with a specific audio cue (e.g., "sit," "stay," "come"). By using consistent verbal cues, your puppy will start to associate certain

words with specific actions. Over time, they'll recognize these cues and respond accordingly, even without the need for physical guidance. If you find it difficult to consistently provide verbal commands during training, you can record your voice using a phone or audio device and play it back during training sessions. This can be a helpful way to reinforce commands if you're training in different environments.

- **Remote Training Devices**
  While not necessary for every dog owner, remote training devices such as clickers with remote triggers or remote training collars can be helpful for more advanced training or certain behavioral issues. For example, a remote training collar allows you to correct unwanted behaviors from a distance, especially during off-leash training or outdoor sessions. However, it's important to use these devices responsibly and under the guidance of a professional trainer to avoid misuse. Remote training tools should always be paired with positive reinforcement and should never be used as a substitute for consistency, patience, and kindness in your puppy's training.

- **Voice Assistants and Smart Devices**

  With the rise of voice assistants like *Amazon Alexa* or *Google Assistant*, it's becoming easier to integrate training commands into everyday life. You can use your voice assistant to create reminders for training sessions, set timers for specific behaviors (e.g., "sit for 10 seconds"), or even ask for training tips. Smart cameras and pet monitoring devices, such as the *Furbo* or *Petcube*, allow you to observe and interact with your puppy when you're not home, helping you monitor progress and offer virtual rewards or verbal cues. While these devices aren't strictly necessary, they can add an extra layer of convenience and flexibility to your training routine.

Conclusion

Technology offers a wealth of tools that can make puppy training more efficient, flexible, and fun. Whether you're using apps and videos for quick tips, taking virtual training classes for personalized guidance, or incorporating audio cues and remote training devices, technology can help streamline your training process and keep your puppy engaged. By integrating these tools into your training routine, you can enhance your puppy's learning experience, track their progress, and overcome challenges with expert advice at your fingertips. With the right combination of digital tools and consistent effort, you'll be well on your way to raising a happy, well-trained puppy, even in a busy world.

Creating Positive Reinforcement Systems

Positive reinforcement is one of the most effective and humane training methods for teaching your puppy desirable behaviors. By rewarding good actions with treats, praise, or play, you create a clear connection between the behavior and the reward. This encourages your puppy to repeat those behaviors, ultimately helping them become well-trained and well-behaved. However, using positive reinforcement effectively requires some understanding of how rewards work, the timing of those rewards, and the importance of keeping things interesting for your puppy. In this section, we'll explore how to create a strong positive reinforcement system that keeps your puppy motivated and engaged throughout their training.

1. Understanding How to Use Treats and Praise Effectively

Treats and praise are two of the most powerful tools in your positive reinforcement toolkit. Both serve as rewards for desired behaviors, but using them correctly and at the right time is essential for effective training.

- **Timing is Key**

  One of the most important aspects of positive reinforcement is timing. To ensure your puppy understands what behavior they're being rewarded for, you must offer the treat or praise immediately after the behavior occurs. This immediate feedback helps your puppy make the connection between their action (e.g., sitting, staying, coming when called) and the reward they receive. The longer you wait to offer a reward, the less effective it will be, as your puppy may not associate it with the behavior you want to reinforce.

- **Treats as Primary Reinforcers**

  Treats are an excellent motivator, especially during the early stages of training. Puppies learn quickly when they associate good behavior with a tasty reward. Use high-value treats that your puppy finds irresistible (small bits of cheese, chicken, or commercial training treats work well). Avoid overfeeding and use small portions to keep the rewards meaningful without upsetting your puppy's stomach. Treats should always be given immediately after the correct behavior, ensuring the connection between the action and the reward is clear.

- **Praise as a Secondary Reinforcer**
  While treats are a powerful motivator, verbal praise or affection can also play a crucial role in reinforcing your puppy's behavior. Praise can be just as valuable as treats, especially when combined with physical affection or a happy, excited tone of voice. For example, saying "Good boy!" or "Yes!" in a cheerful, encouraging voice right after your puppy follows a command will reinforce the behavior without relying solely on food. Praise can also be helpful during less critical moments of training or as a backup reward when treats aren't available.

2. The Concept of Intermittent Rewards to Encourage Consistency and Interest

In order to keep your puppy motivated and prevent them from becoming bored or complacent, it's important to incorporate intermittent rewards into your training routine. This concept, also known as variable reinforcement, involves rewarding behaviors at unpredictable intervals, which increases the likelihood that your puppy will continue performing the behavior.

- **Shaping Behavior with Intermittent Rewards**

  In the early stages of training, you'll likely use frequent rewards to teach your puppy a new behavior (such as rewarding them every time they sit on command). However, once your puppy starts to understand the command, you can begin to reduce the frequency of treats and switch to intermittent rewards. This means rewarding your puppy randomly or only after they've completed the desired behavior a certain number of times. This keeps them engaged and excited, as they never quite know when the reward will come.

- **Preventing Dependence on Constant Rewards**

  One common mistake in puppy training is to rely too heavily on treats for every successful behavior, which can lead to a situation where your puppy only behaves well when there's food involved. Intermittent reinforcement helps prevent this by gradually phasing out constant rewards. As your puppy's behavior becomes more reliable, you can reward them less frequently with treats and rely more on praise, toys, or other forms of reinforcement. Over time, this creates a habit of good behavior that isn't solely dependent on food.

- **Keeping Training Fun and Engaging**

  Intermittent rewards also help to maintain your puppy's interest in training. Dogs, like people, can become bored with repetitive routines, especially if the rewards are predictable. By mixing up the rewards (sometimes a treat, other times praise, or occasionally a toy), you keep the training sessions exciting and your puppy's focus sharp. This unpredictability can help sustain motivation, as your puppy will eagerly anticipate the reward without knowing exactly when it will come.

3. Using Your Puppy's Favorite Toys or Games as Training Rewards

While treats and praise are essential, incorporating your puppy's favorite toys and games as rewards can add an extra layer of fun to your training sessions. This approach not only engages your puppy's mind and body but also strengthens the bond between you and your puppy, making training a more enjoyable and interactive experience.

- **Toys as a Positive Reinforcer**
  Some puppies are more motivated by play than food. If you've noticed that your puppy lights up at the sight of a certain toy or enjoys tug-of-war, fetch, or other games, use these toys as rewards during training. For example, after your puppy successfully follows a command (such as "sit" or "down"), you can reward them with a few minutes of their favorite game. This not only provides a mental and physical outlet for your puppy but also strengthens their association between good behavior and enjoyable activities.

- **Interactive Play for Active Puppies**
  For active puppies, incorporating toys that require problem-solving or physical activity can serve as a great reward. Puzzle toys, treat-dispensing toys, or games that involve running and jumping (like fetch or tug-of-war) help keep your puppy engaged and provide a mental workout. You can use these toys to encourage your puppy to focus on commands, like fetching a ball when you say "fetch" or tugging when you say "tug." These types of games can also be a good way to burn off excess energy, making training sessions more effective and enjoyable for both of you.

- **Games as an Engaging Alternative to Treats**
  Some puppies, especially those that may have food sensitivities or are not very food-driven, may prefer toys or games over treats. Offering a favorite toy or playtime can be just as rewarding as food for these pups. Tug-of-war games or fetch sessions can be used to reinforce commands like "drop it," "leave it," or "fetch," turning training into a more dynamic and exciting activity. As with treats, it's important to make sure that playtime is used as a reward only

after the desired behavior has occurred, helping your puppy understand the connection between their actions and the game.

Conclusion

Creating an effective positive reinforcement system is a powerful way to shape your puppy's behavior. By understanding how to use treats, praise, and play effectively, you can motivate your puppy to learn and build a strong, trusting relationship. Combining frequent rewards early on with intermittent reinforcement as training progresses helps keep your puppy engaged and prevents boredom. Additionally, using your puppy's favorite toys and games as rewards provides a fun, interactive element that not only encourages good behavior but strengthens your bond. By using positive reinforcement consistently and creatively, you can ensure your puppy grows into a well-behaved, happy companion who is eager to learn and please.

Chapter 2

The Power of Short, Focused Training Sessions

The Science Behind Short Sessions

Training a puppy can sometimes feel like a daunting task, especially when you're balancing a busy schedule. However, the good news is that your puppy doesn't need hours of training every day to learn effectively. In fact, short, frequent training sessions are often more beneficial than long, drawn-out ones. Understanding how puppies learn, their attention span, and how to structure your training sessions will help you create a routine that's both effective and manageable. In this section, we'll explore why short training sessions are so effective for puppies and how they can lead to better long-term results.

1. How Puppies Learn Best in Short, Frequent Bursts

Puppies, like young children, have a limited ability to focus for extended periods. Their brains are still developing, and they absorb information most effectively when it's presented in small, manageable chunks. Short training sessions cater to how puppies naturally learn and help them retain new information better than if they were forced to concentrate for long periods.

- **Optimal Learning Window**
  Research shows that puppies (and dogs in general) learn best when training sessions are brief and focused. This is because puppies have a limited capacity for cognitive processing, and they can become mentally fatigued if sessions are too long. A 10-minute session allows your puppy to stay engaged, absorb the new information, and be rewarded for their effort without feeling overwhelmed or frustrated. Short bursts of training are far more effective than one long session, which can result in your puppy zoning out, losing interest, or becoming restless.

- **Repetition Reinforces Learning**
  Short, frequent training sessions provide an excellent opportunity to reinforce desired behaviors through repetition. Since puppies learn through repetition, shorter sessions (spread out throughout the day) allow you to reinforce the same behavior multiple times in a way that is

manageable for both you and your puppy. These repeated, positive learning experiences help solidify the connection between a specific action (such as "sit" or "stay") and the reward that follows.

- **Building Consistency**
  Consistency is key to successful training, and shorter, frequent sessions allow you to practice the same behavior several times a day. For example, instead of one hour-long training session, you can practice short 5 to 10-minute sessions throughout the day. This approach ensures that your puppy remains focused and motivated, and it helps them make clear associations between the behavior and the reward. Over time, this repeated exposure leads to long-term learning and progress.

2. Understanding Their Attention Span and Why Less is More

Puppies have shorter attention spans than adult dogs, which is something every puppy owner must keep in mind. Understanding your puppy's attention span and why "less is more" will help you create more effective and enjoyable training sessions.

- **The 5-Minute Rule**

  A common guideline is that puppies can generally focus for about 5 minutes per month of age. So, a 3-month-old puppy may only be able to focus for about 15 minutes, while a 6-month-old puppy may have an attention span of around 30 minutes. However, this doesn't mean that your puppy should be expected to train for these full durations—especially not all at once. Most puppies will begin to lose interest and become distracted well before they reach their maximum attention span. Keeping training sessions at or under 10 minutes ensures that your puppy remains focused, avoids burnout, and has the best chance to succeed.

- **Avoiding Overload**

  When training sessions are too long, your puppy may start to feel overwhelmed or frustrated. This can lead to disengagement, resistance, and even anxiety around training. Puppies can only process so much information at once, and if you try to teach them too many new things in one session, they may not retain the lesson. Short sessions allow for more manageable information absorption, preventing your puppy from feeling overloaded while still getting plenty of practice.

- **Building Positive Associations**
  Keeping training sessions short also ensures that your puppy associates training with positive, enjoyable experiences. If you push your puppy to focus for too long, training can quickly become a chore for them. However, short sessions followed by rewards (treats, praise, play) help your puppy build a positive association with the training process, making them more eager to participate and learn in the future.

3. The Benefits of a Focused 10-Minute Routine Versus Longer, Overwhelming Sessions

There's a clear difference between a focused, short training session and a long, draining one. Although it may seem like longer sessions would lead to faster results, research and experience show that short, concentrated training bursts are much more effective in the long run. Here's why:

- **Better Focus and Retention**
  A focused 10-minute training session encourages your puppy to give you their full attention without getting distracted or exhausted. When

your puppy is engaged, they're more likely to retain what they've learned. Longer sessions, on the other hand, can lead to scattered attention, fatigue, and frustration, which ultimately reduces the effectiveness of the session. By keeping things brief and to the point, you can ensure that each minute counts.

- **Reduced Risk of Burnout**
  Just like humans, puppies can experience mental fatigue. If a session is too long, they may start to disengage, which could make them resistant to future training attempts. Short, regular sessions, however, keep your puppy energized and motivated to participate. They'll be more excited for the next session because they won't feel burned out. This helps maintain a consistent training schedule, which is key to long-term success.

- **Easier to Fit into a Busy Schedule**
  One of the most important benefits of short training sessions is that they're easy to incorporate into your daily routine. With just 10 minutes a day, you can fit in a productive training session without disrupting your schedule. Whether it's right after a walk, before

meals, or during a break in your day, short training sessions are flexible enough to work around your busy lifestyle. You don't need to block off large chunks of time for training—just 10 minutes here and there, spread out over the day, can lead to impressive results.

Conclusion

Short, focused training sessions are the key to effective puppy training. Understanding your puppy's attention span and structuring training in frequent, bite-sized bursts helps them learn without feeling overwhelmed or fatigued. A 10-minute routine not only maximizes your puppy's focus and retention but also makes training easier to incorporate into your busy schedule. By embracing the science behind short sessions, you're setting your puppy up for long-term success and creating positive, enjoyable training experiences that will benefit both you and your puppy.

Timing and Frequency

When it comes to puppy training, one of the most important factors in achieving success is the timing and frequency of your sessions. Training doesn't need to take up large chunks of time or require hours of effort; instead, frequent, short bursts of training throughout the day can be just as effective—if not more so. By strategically timing your training sessions and taking advantage of spare moments in your day, you can create a routine that fits seamlessly into your busy lifestyle while still making meaningful progress. In this section, we'll explore the optimal frequency of training sessions, how to incorporate training into your daily routine, and how to structure your day for maximum efficiency.

1. The Optimal Frequency of Short Sessions Throughout the Day

Rather than squeezing in one long training session, frequent, shorter sessions spread throughout the day are more effective for your puppy's learning and retention. Frequent repetition of commands and behaviors helps reinforce positive habits, while also keeping training engaging and manageable for both you and your puppy.

- **Multiple Sessions for Consistency**
  Research and experience show that training your puppy multiple times a day (ideally 3-5 short sessions) is more effective than cramming everything into one long stretch. These frequent sessions provide plenty of opportunities for your puppy to practice and reinforce behaviors in a

consistent, manageable way. By breaking up training into several mini-sessions, you ensure that your puppy doesn't get mentally fatigued, and you maintain their interest in the process.

- **Maximizing Learning Through Repetition**
  Puppies thrive on repetition, and short, frequent sessions provide an ideal way to offer this repetition without overwhelming them. By practicing commands and behaviors multiple times a day, you ensure that the connections between actions and rewards are reinforced regularly. This helps your puppy retain what they're learning and improve their responses faster than if they only practiced a behavior once a day.

- **Building a Habit**
  Frequent, short training sessions also help your puppy develop a habit of learning and responding to commands throughout the day. When training becomes a regular part of their routine, your puppy will start to expect it and even enjoy it. This consistency helps your puppy understand that certain behaviors are always expected of them, leading to smoother and faster learning in the long run.

2. How to Make the Most of Spare Moments (e.g., Before Meals, While Waiting for the Bus)

One of the biggest challenges of puppy training for busy people is finding time to practice. But you'd be surprised at how many opportunities exist throughout the day to work with your puppy in small bursts—if you know how to take advantage of them. By using "spare moments" in your day, you can sneak in quick training sessions that don't require you to carve out extra time.

- **Training Before Meals**
  Mealtime is an excellent time to practice commands like "sit," "stay," and "wait." Before putting your puppy's food bowl down, ask them to perform a command like "sit" and reward them with their meal. This not only teaches your puppy to be patient and disciplined, but it also helps reinforce the connection between following a command and receiving a reward. You can do this in just a minute or two, making it a perfect example of a quick training session.

- **Waiting for the Bus or Car**
  Any time you find yourself waiting—whether it's for the bus, while you're in the car, or even while standing in line at the grocery store—is a

great opportunity to practice training. For example, while waiting in the car, you can practice "sit" or "stay," or during a break at the bus stop, you can work on leash manners. These short sessions are especially useful for reinforcing basic commands like "sit," "down," or "watch me." The key is to use any idle time as an opportunity for training, turning everyday moments into productive learning sessions.

- **During Walks or Playtime**
  Walks and play sessions are ideal times to incorporate training without disrupting the flow of your day. While walking your puppy, use moments of downtime—like when you're waiting at a crosswalk or taking a break—to reinforce commands like "heel," "sit," or "leave it." Playtime with your puppy is another opportunity to sneak in training, especially if your puppy loves fetch or tug-of-war. Use these games to reinforce basic obedience skills, such as "drop it," "fetch," or "bring it." Incorporating training during these everyday activities makes the process more enjoyable for your puppy, and it keeps training sessions short and manageable.

3. Creating a Simple Training Plan with Multiple 10-Minute Intervals

One of the easiest ways to ensure your puppy gets enough training while still managing your busy schedule is to create a simple plan with multiple 10-minute training intervals. The key is to be consistent, make use of your available time, and keep training sessions focused and short. With this approach, you can easily fit training into your routine without feeling overwhelmed.

- **Structured, Bite-Sized Sessions**
  Start by planning 2-4 10-minute training sessions throughout the day, focusing on a specific behavior or command in each session. For example, one session could focus on "sit," while another could work on "down" or leash manners. Having a clear goal for each session helps you stay focused and ensures that your puppy gets the attention they need for each skill. You can keep a training log to track progress, noting what you worked on in each session and any improvements or challenges.

- **Morning, Midday, and Evening Sessions**
  A great way to spread training throughout the day is to schedule training sessions at different

times—such as in the morning before work, during your lunch break, and in the evening after dinner. These "anchor points" in your day give you natural breaks to practice with your puppy. For example, a morning session could focus on leash walking, the midday session could reinforce "sit" and "stay," and the evening session might be dedicated to basic obedience commands like "come" or "down." This schedule helps maintain consistency and ensures your puppy gets multiple chances to learn.

- **Plan Around Your Schedule**
  If your schedule is particularly hectic, don't worry about setting a rigid plan. Instead, work with the flow of your day. If you miss a session, it's okay—just make sure you catch up later in the day. The flexibility of short sessions makes it easy to adapt to your routine without adding extra stress. The goal is to maintain consistency in your training, even if that means sometimes doing 2-3 sessions in a row or fitting them in whenever you find a free moment. The more you make training a natural part of your day, the more successful you'll be.

Conclusion

Effective training doesn't require long hours; in fact, short, frequent sessions are the best way to ensure your puppy stays focused, engaged, and excited to learn. By scheduling multiple 10-minute intervals throughout the day, you'll not only maximize your puppy's learning potential but also seamlessly integrate training into your daily routine. Whether it's before meals, during a walk, or while waiting for the bus, there are countless moments throughout the day that can be turned into productive training opportunities. With a little creativity and consistency, you'll be well on your way to a well-trained, happy puppy without the stress of long, overwhelming training sessions.

Keeping It Fun and Engaging

Training your puppy should be a rewarding and enjoyable experience, not just for your puppy but for you as well. If training becomes monotonous or frustrating, it's easy to lose motivation, and your puppy may begin to disengage or even associate training with negative feelings. However, when training is fun, positive, and engaging, both you and your puppy will look forward to the sessions. In this section, we'll explore how to keep training lighthearted and enjoyable, how to prevent boredom, and why enthusiasm and praise play such a vital role in maintaining your puppy's interest and motivation.

1. How to Keep Training Positive and Enjoyable for Both You and Your Puppy

A positive training experience not only helps your puppy learn faster but also strengthens the bond between the two of you. When you maintain a positive attitude and create an enjoyable environment for learning, your puppy is more likely to stay engaged and motivated. Here's how to do it:

- **Set Realistic Expectations**
  One of the easiest ways to keep training enjoyable is by setting realistic goals and expectations. Puppies are learning at their own pace, so avoid placing too much pressure on them or yourself. Celebrate small wins and milestones, no matter how minor they may seem. For example, if your puppy successfully sits for a second when asked, praise them enthusiastically—even if they don't stay in place for long. These small successes build momentum and create a positive feedback loop that encourages your puppy to keep trying.

- **Use a Playful Tone and Body Language**

  Puppies respond well to cheerful, upbeat tones. When you're training, keep your voice happy and encouraging. You don't have to be overly loud, but enthusiasm in your voice will excite your puppy and make training feel like a fun game rather than a chore. Use your body language to convey excitement, too—squatting down to their level, clapping your hands, or jumping around a little will grab their attention and make them more engaged in the training.

- **End on a High Note**

  To keep your puppy looking forward to future training sessions, always end each session on a positive note. If they've mastered a behavior or shown improvement, reward them and then finish with a play session or a few minutes of praise. Ending on a high note will leave your puppy feeling accomplished and eager for the next session. If things haven't gone well, it's okay to call it a day early, reward them for their effort, and try again next time. This way, your puppy won't associate training with stress or failure, but with fun and success.

2. Mixing Up Activities to Prevent Boredom and Reinforce Interest

Puppies, like children, can easily become bored with repetitive activities. If you do the same routine over and over, training can feel like a drag for your puppy, and you may start to lose their attention. Mixing things up keeps training fresh and exciting. Here's how you can keep things interesting:

- **Vary the Commands and Behaviors**
  While consistency is key in training, you can also add variety by rotating through different commands and behaviors during each session. For example, one day you might focus on "sit," "stay," and "down," and another day you could work on "come," "leave it," and "fetch." Changing up the routine not only keeps your puppy's interest but also strengthens their overall obedience by practicing a range of skills. Just be sure to keep it simple and focus on one or two new behaviors at a time.

- **Incorporate Play into Training**
  Training doesn't have to be limited to sit-stay-come drills. You can make training more fun by turning it into a game. For example, teach your

puppy to play "hide and seek" by hiding a treat or toy and having them "find it." Or, turn recall ("come") into a game of tug-of-war or fetch. These activities combine physical exercise with mental stimulation and help reinforce training in a more dynamic way. Playing games also allows your puppy to let off steam, making them more likely to stay focused during the next training session.

- **Introduce New Training Tools or Environments**
  Every now and then, change the environment where you're training. If you've been working indoors, take your training outside for a fresh experience. Try practicing commands in the backyard, at the park, or even while on a walk. You can also introduce different training tools, like a new toy or a clicker, to keep things exciting. Switching things up challenges your puppy to generalize the commands they've learned in different contexts, reinforcing their skills in new ways.

3. The Importance of Enthusiasm and Praise in Motivating Your Puppy

Your puppy looks to you for guidance, and your energy plays a huge role in their motivation. The more enthusiastic you are during training, the more excited your puppy will be to participate. Positive reinforcement in the form of praise is equally important in keeping your puppy motivated and building a strong, trusting relationship.

- **Enthusiasm is Contagious**
  Just like humans, puppies feed off of the energy around them. If you approach training with excitement, your puppy will respond in kind. Be animated and upbeat when giving commands, and celebrate their successes with high-energy praise. Jump, cheer, or speak in a happy, animated voice when they get something right. This positive energy makes training fun, increases your puppy's eagerness to learn, and reinforces their connection to you as a source of joy and reward.

- **Verbal Praise as a Reward**
  Positive reinforcement isn't limited to treats and toys. Verbal praise is an incredibly powerful tool

in motivating your puppy. Phrases like "Good girl!" or "Yes!" delivered in a happy, excited tone let your puppy know that they've done something right and reinforce the behavior. Keep your praise genuine and enthusiastic. Puppies are very perceptive, and they can tell when you're truly excited about their progress. This kind of reinforcement builds confidence and helps your puppy understand what they're being rewarded for.

- **Physical Affection and Play**
  In addition to verbal praise, physical affection (such as petting, cuddling, or belly rubs) and play are powerful motivators. After a successful training session, spend a few moments interacting with your puppy in a positive, affectionate way. If your puppy enjoys toys, incorporate them into the training session as a reward for good behavior. These affectionate rewards not only strengthen the bond between you and your puppy but also motivate them to engage in training because they associate it with positive outcomes.

Conclusion

Training should be a fun and enjoyable experience for both you and your puppy. By keeping the sessions positive, mixing up activities to prevent boredom, and infusing each training moment with enthusiasm and praise, you'll create a productive and engaging learning environment. When you and your puppy enjoy the process, training becomes less of a task and more of a rewarding opportunity to bond and grow together. Keep things lighthearted, celebrate small successes, and make training an exciting part of your daily routine—your puppy will be eager to learn, and you'll both benefit from the process.

Teaching 'Sit'

Teaching your puppy to sit is one of the first and most important behaviors you can introduce, as it lays the foundation for other commands and helps establish good manners. Fortunately, "sit" is one of the easiest behaviors to teach and can be accomplished with just a few simple techniques and a little patience. In this section, we'll explore the step-by-step process of teaching your puppy to sit on command, how to use treats as a reward and guide, and the importance of consistency in your voice commands and hand signals.

1. Simple Techniques to Teach Your Puppy to Sit on Command

The "sit" command is a fundamental obedience skill that helps your puppy learn self-control and focus. It's also a great way to start building a strong foundation of trust and communication between you and your puppy. Here's a simple, step-by-step method for teaching "sit."

- **Get Your Puppy's Attention**
  Start by ensuring that your puppy is focused on you and ready to engage. Hold a treat in your hand to grab their attention and make sure they're interested. This will help them focus on you during the training session.

- **Guide with a Treat**
  Hold the treat close to your puppy's nose and slowly move your hand upwards, just above their head. As your puppy looks up to follow the treat, their bottom will naturally lower toward the ground. Most puppies instinctively sit down as they try to focus on the treat. Once their bottom touches the floor, immediately say the command "sit" in a clear, happy voice, and give them the treat as a reward.

- **Repeat and Reward**

  Repeat this process several times, each time using the treat to guide them into the sitting position. Make sure to reward them with praise and a treat immediately after they sit. Puppies learn best when they are rewarded for their efforts, so prompt and consistent rewards help reinforce the behavior.

- **Introduce the Verbal Command**

  Once your puppy starts sitting consistently when you guide them with the treat, start saying the word "sit" just as they begin to sit. Say it in a calm, clear tone, and pair it with the motion of the treat guiding them into position. Eventually, your puppy will begin to associate the sound of the word "sit" with the action of sitting.

2. Using Treats to Guide and Reward the Behavior

Treats are a powerful tool in teaching new behaviors, especially for puppies. They serve as an immediate reward that reinforces the desired behavior, helping your puppy make the connection between the action (sitting) and the reward (treat). Here's how to effectively use treats in training:

- **Use High-Value Treats**

  Choose small, tasty treats that your puppy really loves, especially when you're just starting out. High-value treats (like pieces of chicken or cheese) can make the training process more exciting for your puppy and keep them engaged. Reserve these special treats for training sessions, so your puppy will quickly learn that good things happen when they participate.

- **Timing is Key**

  Timing is crucial when rewarding your puppy for sitting. You want to give the treat immediately after your puppy sits so they can associate the action with the reward. If you delay the treat, your puppy may not connect the reward to the desired behavior, making the training less effective. As soon as their bottom touches the ground, say "sit" and immediately reward them with a treat.

- **Gradually Fade the Treats**

  While treats are an essential part of positive reinforcement, the goal is to eventually reduce your reliance on them. Once your puppy reliably sits on command, start to fade out the treats by offering them intermittently. You can begin by rewarding with treats only some of the time and gradually shift to offering praise or petting as rewards. This helps your puppy understand that while treats are great, they should also respond to verbal praise and other forms of reward.

3. Ensuring Consistency in Your Hand Signals and Voice Commands

Consistency is one of the most important factors in effective puppy training. Using the same hand signal and verbal cue each time ensures that your puppy understands exactly what you want them to do. This will make learning faster and help avoid confusion.

- **Use a Consistent Hand Signal**
  Many puppies learn hand signals faster than verbal cues, so it's important to choose a simple, consistent hand motion to accompany your verbal command. For "sit," most trainers use a single upward motion of the hand, holding the treat above the puppy's nose to guide them into the sitting position. Keep this hand signal the same every time you practice, so your puppy can start associating the movement with the action.

- **Clear and Consistent Verbal Command**
  Choose a short, clear verbal cue like "sit" and use

it consistently. Say the word the same way every time you want your puppy to perform the behavior. If you say "sit" in different tones or with varying inflections, your puppy might become confused about what you mean. Keep your tone friendly, upbeat, and firm, but avoid shouting or using a harsh voice. Positive, consistent cues make it easier for your puppy to understand and respond.

- **Practice in Different Environments**
  While it's important to practice the "sit" command in a quiet, controlled environment (like your living room), don't forget to reinforce it in different settings as well. Once your puppy starts to sit reliably in one place, try practicing in different areas of the house, outside in the yard, or even at the park. This helps your puppy generalize the behavior and understand that "sit" means the same thing no matter where they are. Keep the hand signal and verbal command consistent across all environments to reinforce the connection.

Conclusion

Teaching your puppy to sit is a simple but powerful first step in establishing good behavior and communication. By using treats to guide and reward your puppy, maintaining consistency in your hand signals and voice commands, and practicing in different environments, you'll help your puppy learn this essential command quickly and effectively. Remember that patience and positive reinforcement are key—training should always be fun and rewarding for both you and your puppy. With time and consistency, your puppy will not only learn how to sit on command but also develop a stronger understanding of how to respond to other cues and behaviors.

Teaching 'Stay'

The "stay" command is an important skill that helps your puppy learn self-control and patience. It's also a great way to prevent your puppy from running off or getting into dangerous situations when you need them to remain in place. Like all training, teaching "stay" requires patience, consistency, and positive reinforcement. In this section, we'll break down how to teach your puppy the "stay" command, how to use visual and verbal cues to encourage them, and how to gradually increase the duration and distance to reinforce the behavior.

1. Breaking Down the 'Stay' Command into Manageable Steps

The "stay" command may seem simple, but it involves both physical and mental discipline for your puppy. The key is to break the behavior down into smaller steps, allowing your puppy to gradually build up their ability to remain in place. Here's how to introduce the "stay" command in a manageable way:

- **Start with 'Sit' or 'Down'**
  Before teaching "stay," your puppy should already be familiar with basic commands like "sit" or "down." These positions give your puppy a stable foundation to stay in place. Start by asking your puppy to either sit or lie down, as these positions are most conducive to the "stay" behavior.

- **Introduce the 'Stay' Cue**
  Once your puppy is sitting or lying down, calmly say the command "stay" and hold your hand out in front of them, palm facing them as a visual cue. The "stay" hand signal is similar to a "stop" gesture, with your fingers pointing

upward. Initially, you can keep your hand close to their nose to help reinforce the command. Keep your voice calm and firm, and avoid over-exaggerating or shouting the word "stay." It should be clear, confident, and consistent.

- **Reward Immediate Compliance**
  If your puppy stays in position for even a moment, immediately reward them with praise or a treat. This reinforces the connection between the "stay" command and the positive outcome. You'll gradually increase the length of time before you reward them as they begin to grasp the concept. It's essential to reward every attempt in the early stages, even if they only stay for a second or two.

2. Using Visual and Verbal Cues to Encourage a Puppy to Remain in Place

While the "stay" command relies heavily on verbal cues, puppies are also very responsive to visual signals. By combining both visual and verbal cues, you can make the "stay" command more effective and easier for your puppy to understand. Here's how to use both types of cues:

- **Verbal Cue ('Stay')** Use a calm, steady voice when giving the verbal cue "stay." Be firm, but not harsh. The key is consistency—say the word "stay" in the same tone every time to avoid confusing your puppy. Puppies learn better when cues are predictable, so avoid using variations like "hold still" or "don't move." Stick with one clear command, and only say it once to avoid reinforcing a habit of repeated commands.

- **Visual Cue (Hand Signal)** Along with the verbal cue, use a visual signal to help your puppy understand the "stay" command. The most common hand signal for "stay" is an open hand with the palm facing outwards, as if signaling "stop." This gesture is universal and easily recognizable by puppies. Start by holding your hand out in front of your puppy's face while they are sitting or lying down, then gradually reduce the proximity of your hand to their nose as they learn to remain in place. Your puppy will learn that the hand signal and the verbal command work together to convey the message.

- **Consistency is Key** When teaching "stay," be consistent in how you use both cues. Always use the same hand signal and verbal command in the same way. Inconsistent cues may confuse your puppy and delay the learning process. Use the same tone of voice, and ensure your hand signal is always presented in a clear, understandable manner.

3. Gradually Increasing the Duration and Distance to Reinforce the Behavior

The ultimate goal of teaching "stay" is for your puppy to remain in place for longer periods and at greater distances. However, this can take time, so it's important to gradually increase the duration and distance of the "stay" in manageable steps. Here's how to reinforce the behavior over time:

- **Start with Short Duration**
  Initially, only ask your puppy to stay for a few seconds. After they successfully stay in position for a brief moment, immediately reward them with praise or a treat. The focus here is on building the foundation of the "stay" behavior, so make sure your puppy is successful at each stage before moving on to longer durations.

- **Increase Duration Gradually**
  Once your puppy consistently stays in position for a few seconds, you can begin increasing the duration. Add one or two seconds at a time, and always reward them for staying the full time. If

your puppy starts to break the stay before the set duration, calmly reset them to the "sit" or "down" position, and try again with a shorter duration. This way, you ensure that your puppy learns to stay in place until released, without feeling overwhelmed.

- **Increase Distance Slowly**
  After your puppy can reliably stay in place for a few seconds, start introducing distance. Begin by taking one step back, and then return quickly to reward them for staying. Gradually increase the number of steps you take away from your puppy while still rewarding them for staying.

  Eventually, you can work up to leaving the room for a few moments, but always go slowly. If your puppy breaks the stay before you return, go back to a shorter distance, and reinforce their success. Distance and duration should be added at a pace that your puppy is comfortable with, allowing them to remain successful at each stage.

Conclusion

Teaching your puppy to stay is a critical command that promotes patience, focus, and self-control. By breaking the behavior into manageable steps, using clear verbal and visual cues, and gradually increasing both duration and distance, you'll help your puppy master the "stay" command with ease. Consistency, patience, and positive reinforcement are key—keep sessions short, fun, and rewarding, and your puppy will soon learn to stay in place reliably. Over time, this simple command will help your puppy become more well-mannered, and it will lay the groundwork for other essential behaviors.

Teaching 'Come'

The "come" command is one of the most important behaviors you can teach your puppy. It's a life-saving command that helps you bring your puppy to you in any situation, whether they're off-leash, distracted, or running away. A strong recall ensures safety and fosters a good relationship between you and your puppy. The key to success with "come" is to make it fun and rewarding, practice in various environments, and gradually build reliability even in the face of distractions. In this section, we'll break down how to teach "come" as a fun game, practice it in different locations, and address distractions to ensure your puppy comes every time.

1. Making 'Come' a Fun Game with Positive Rewards

The best way to teach your puppy to come is by making it a game that's enjoyable for them. Puppies are naturally playful and eager to engage, so turning the recall command into a fun experience makes them more likely to want to respond. Here's how to make the "come" command exciting and rewarding for your puppy:

- **Use High-Value Rewards**
  To make "come" more enticing, use high-value treats that your puppy loves, such as small pieces of chicken, cheese, or their favorite toy. The more rewarding the reward, the more likely your puppy will be to come running when called. Make sure the treats are small enough that your puppy can quickly eat them, allowing for a smooth and fast reward, but tasty enough that your puppy is motivated to work for them.

- **Exciting Voice and Body Language**
  When you call your puppy to come, use a high-energy, enthusiastic tone. Puppies respond well to a happy, upbeat voice, so make the command sound exciting and inviting. You can also clap your hands, crouch down to their level, or run

backward a few steps to encourage your puppy to chase after you. By using energetic body language and an excited tone, you'll make "come" feel like a fun game and motivate your puppy to respond quickly.

- **Reward Immediately and Generously**
  Once your puppy comes to you, reward them right away with lots of praise, petting, and the treat or toy. Be sure to celebrate their success to reinforce that coming to you leads to good things. If you wait too long to give the reward, your puppy might not make the connection between their action (coming to you) and the reward. The sooner you give the reward, the clearer it is for your puppy that they've done the right thing.

2. How to Practice the Recall Command in Different Locations and Situations

One of the most important aspects of teaching "come" is practicing it in a variety of environments and situations. This ensures that your puppy can reliably respond no matter where they are or what else is going on. Here's how to make sure your puppy generalizes the recall command:

- **Start in a Quiet, Controlled Environment**
  Begin practicing "come" in a quiet, distraction-free area like your living room or backyard. Start by calling your puppy to you from a short distance. When they come, immediately reward them with praise and a treat. This will give your puppy the chance to learn the command without getting distracted by other sights, sounds, or smells.

- **Gradually Increase the Challenge**
  Once your puppy has learned to come to you reliably in a calm setting, begin to add more distractions. Move to different areas of the yard, the park, or other safe outdoor spaces where there are more sights, sounds, and smells. Start with shorter distances and gradually increase the distance as your puppy becomes more confident in responding. For example, call them from one side of the yard and reward them when they come to you.

- **Practice During Walks and Outdoor Adventures**
  Incorporating the "come" command into daily activities, such as walks, hikes, or trips to the park, helps your puppy learn to respond reliably

even when they are distracted by new sights, sounds, and smells. On a leash, gently call your puppy to come, and reward them when they do. Start with short distances and gradually increase the distance over time, ensuring your puppy responds each time. This also builds trust between you and your puppy, as they will associate the "come" command with positive experiences in real-world situations.

3. Addressing Distractions and Ensuring Your Puppy Comes Every Time

It's essential that your puppy learns to come when called, no matter what else is going on around them. This means practicing with distractions and gradually building their focus and reliability. Here's how to address distractions and make sure your puppy comes every time:

- **Start with Low-Level Distractions**
  When your puppy is learning to come, start practicing in environments with minimal distractions. Gradually introduce more distractions as your puppy becomes more comfortable with the command. This can include practicing around toys, other people, or even other dogs (on a leash). Each time your

puppy successfully comes despite the distraction, reward them generously to reinforce that listening to the recall command is always the right choice.

- **Use a Long Leash for Greater Control**
  When practicing in more distracting environments (like a park or dog-friendly area), use a long leash or training lead to ensure that you have control over your puppy. This will allow you to give them the freedom to explore, while still being able to guide them back to you if they don't respond to the "come" command. A long leash can help prevent them from running off and gives you a chance to correct their behavior if they don't come when called.

- **Be Consistent and Patient**
  The key to building reliability in your puppy's recall is consistency. Always call your puppy to come with the same tone of voice and the same enthusiasm. Don't call them in a neutral or frustrated voice, as this can create confusion. If your puppy doesn't come immediately, don't chase them—simply call them again, and if needed, gently reel them in with the leash. Once they come to you, reward them immediately to

reinforce that coming to you is always the best
choice. With enough repetition and patience,
your puppy will learn that "come" means the
same thing every time, no matter the
distractions.

Conclusion

The "come" command is a vital skill for your puppy's
safety and your peace of mind. By making the training
process fun and rewarding, practicing in a variety of
locations and situations, and gradually addressing
distractions, you can teach your puppy to reliably come
to you every time. Remember, consistency is key—always
reward your puppy for their successful recall, and with
time, your puppy will learn that coming when called is a
rewarding, positive experience. By focusing on positive
reinforcement, patience, and fun, you'll build a strong
foundation for a reliable recall that will keep your puppy
safe and happy in any environment.

Preventing Frustration for Both You and Your Puppy

Training a puppy can be incredibly rewarding, but it can
also be challenging at times. Both you and your puppy
can experience moments of frustration, especially when

progress seems slow or when your puppy gets overwhelmed. The key to maintaining a successful training experience is recognizing when both you and your puppy need a break, adjusting the pace as needed, and celebrating every small victory along the way. In this section, we'll explore how to avoid frustration during training, keep a positive attitude, and ensure that both you and your puppy are set up for success.

1. Recognizing When Your Puppy Is Overwhelmed and Adjusting the Pace

Puppies are highly energetic and eager to learn, but their attention spans are short, and they can become easily overwhelmed. It's important to recognize when your puppy has reached their limit, so you can adjust the pace of your training sessions and keep them motivated.

- **Watch for Signs of Overwhelm**
  Just like young children, puppies can become easily overstimulated or frustrated if they're asked to focus for too long. Signs that your puppy is getting overwhelmed include yawning, turning away from you, losing interest, or becoming overly excitable. If your puppy starts to show these signs, it's a good indication that they need a break. Pushing them too hard can

lead to burnout, confusion, and a negative association with training.

- **Adjust the Length of Training Sessions**
  Instead of trying to push through a session when your puppy is losing focus, shorten the session and make it more manageable. For young puppies, aim for sessions that are 5–10 minutes long, especially when you're introducing new commands. As they grow older and their attention span increases, you can lengthen the sessions slightly, but always keep the sessions upbeat and engaging to maintain their interest.

- **Slow Down When Necessary**
  If your puppy is struggling with a particular command or concept, it's okay to slow the pace of training. Break down the behavior into even smaller steps or revisit previous lessons to reinforce what they've already learned. If progress is slow, don't be discouraged—praise your puppy for their efforts and take time to revisit the basics before moving on to more advanced training.

2. How to Stay Calm and Patient, Even When Progress Feels Slow

Training a puppy takes time, and it's important to remember that they are learning at their own pace. It's easy to get frustrated when progress feels slow, but your patience will pay off in the long run. Staying calm and positive is essential for creating a supportive learning environment for your puppy.

- **Maintain a Positive Mindset**
  Puppies, like people, can pick up on your mood. If you're feeling frustrated, your puppy may become anxious or stressed, which can hinder their ability to learn. Take a deep breath, remind yourself that this is a learning process for both of you, and focus on the progress you've made so far, not just the areas where improvement is needed. Stay positive, and celebrate the small wins along the way.

- **Focus on the Process, Not Just the Outcome**
  It's easy to become fixated on achieving specific training goals quickly, but the process of training itself is just as important as the results. Focus on making training sessions enjoyable and rewarding, both for you and your puppy. Even if

your puppy only gets part of the behavior right, acknowledge their effort and continue reinforcing their progress. Remember, consistency and patience will yield results over time.

- **Use Self-Compassion**
It's natural to feel discouraged at times, but remember to be kind to yourself, too. Puppy training is a journey, and it's okay to make mistakes along the way. If you don't see immediate results, take a step back, reassess your approach, and adjust as needed. Every puppy is different, and they will learn at their own pace. Give yourself credit for the hard work you're putting in, and remember that progress takes time.

3. The Importance of Taking Breaks and Celebrating Small Victories

Training should be a fun, positive experience for both you and your puppy. Taking breaks and celebrating small victories will help keep both of you motivated and excited about the process. Overworking your puppy or yourself can lead to burnout, but frequent breaks and recognition of progress will keep the experience enjoyable and sustainable.

- **Take Regular Breaks**

  Puppies are like sponges—they absorb a lot of information in a short amount of time. However, just like us, they need breaks to process what they've learned and recharge. After a few minutes of training, give your puppy a short break to relax and play. This will prevent mental fatigue and help them stay engaged and focused during future sessions. You can also use this time to reset your own mind and prepare for the next phase of training.

- **Celebrate Every Small Victory**

  Every step of progress counts! Whether your puppy stays for an extra second in the "stay" position, learns to sit on command, or responds to their name, celebrate these small victories with praise, treats, or a quick play session. This positive reinforcement boosts their confidence and motivates them to continue working. The more often you celebrate these moments, the more eager your puppy will be to keep learning.

- **Make Training Fun**

  Keep your training sessions playful and lighthearted. Use games, toys, and lots of excitement to make learning feel like a fun activity. If training feels like a chore, your puppy may start to lose interest, and you may find yourself feeling frustrated. By incorporating games and playful interactions, you can keep both of you motivated and eager to return to the next session.

Conclusion

Preventing frustration is key to successful puppy training. Recognizing when your puppy is overwhelmed, staying calm and patient, and taking regular breaks will help both of you stay on track and motivated. Remember, training is a process, and each step forward, no matter how small, is an achievement. Celebrate those small victories, adjust the pace as needed, and stay focused on making the experience enjoyable for both you and your puppy. By fostering a positive, supportive training environment, you'll lay the foundation for a strong bond and a well-trained, happy puppy.

Avoiding Overtraining

Training a puppy can be an exciting and rewarding experience, but it's important to know when to stop before either you or your puppy becomes exhausted or frustrated. Overtraining can lead to stress, confusion, and even burnout, which will set back your puppy's progress in the long run. Keeping training sessions brief and positive not only helps avoid overtraining but also ensures that your puppy remains enthusiastic and engaged in learning. In this section, we'll explore how to recognize signs of fatigue or stress, how to know when to end a training session, and the long-term benefits of keeping training sessions short and upbeat.

1. Signs That Your Puppy Is Getting Tired or Stressed

Puppies have lots of energy, but they also have limited attention spans and can become overstimulated or tired during training. Recognizing when your puppy is no longer enjoying the session is key to preventing overtraining. Here are some signs to watch for:

- **Yawning or Sniffing Excessively**
  If your puppy starts yawning frequently or sniffing around the area more than usual, it

could be a sign they're becoming tired or mentally exhausted. Puppies often yawn as a way to self-soothe when they're feeling stressed or overstimulated. Excessive sniffing can indicate a loss of focus, which often occurs when they're mentally fatigued.

- **Avoiding Eye Contact or Turning Away**
  A puppy that's starting to disengage may avoid eye contact or turn away from you. This is a sign that they've had enough and need a break. They may also start wandering off or lose interest in the treats and toys that normally motivate them.

- **Pacing or Licking Their Lips**
  Pacing around or licking their lips repeatedly can be signs that your puppy is feeling anxious or stressed. These behaviors indicate that they may be overwhelmed or uncertain, and it's a good idea to stop the session and give them a chance to relax.

- **Stiff Body Language or Growling**
  If your puppy starts to tense up, become stiff, or even growl or whine, it's a clear indication that they're feeling stressed or frustrated. These signals mean that they need a break or a change

in the training approach. Pushing them through these behaviors can lead to negative associations with training.

2. How to Recognize When to Stop a Session and Give Your Puppy a Break

Knowing when to stop a training session is just as important as knowing how to begin. If you push your puppy past their limits, they're less likely to retain the information, and the session will become counterproductive. Here's how to recognize when it's time to end a session:

- **Observe Your Puppy's Behavior**
  Pay close attention to your puppy's body language and behavior throughout the training session. If you notice signs of fatigue, frustration, or disinterest (like the ones mentioned above), it's time to stop. Ending the session on a positive note, when your puppy has successfully completed a command or learned something new, will help them feel good about the training experience.

- **Use the "5-Minute Rule"**
  As a general guideline, keep training sessions short—around 5 to 10 minutes per session,

depending on your puppy's age and energy level. Puppies have shorter attention spans and can become tired quickly. It's better to do multiple brief sessions throughout the day than to try to cram everything into one long session. If you're unsure when to stop, use the "5-minute rule" to help gauge the session length.

- **Watch for Signs of Engagement**
  If your puppy is still actively engaging with you, paying attention, and responding to commands, you can continue the session. However, once they start losing focus, that's a good time to wrap things up. It's important to leave training sessions before your puppy becomes too distracted or exhausted. This way, they'll look forward to the next session instead of feeling drained or overwhelmed.

- **End on a Positive Note**
  Always aim to end each session on a high point. If your puppy successfully performs a command, even if it's just for a few seconds, reward them and finish the session right then. This leaves a positive impression and will help motivate your puppy for the next training session. Puppies are more likely to remember the

last few moments of a training session, so ending on a success will reinforce their good behavior.

3. The Long-Term Benefits of Keeping Training Sessions Brief and Positive

Short, focused training sessions are not only easier for your puppy to handle, but they also come with long-term benefits that will lead to faster, more effective learning. Here's why brief and positive sessions are the way to go:

- **Better Retention and Focus**
  Puppies have limited attention spans, and overloading them with too much information at once can result in confusion or frustration. Short, focused sessions allow your puppy to process what they've learned, making it easier for them to retain the information. By keeping sessions brief, you can ensure that each learning opportunity is fully absorbed, which builds a stronger foundation for future training.

- **Positive Associations with Training**
  Keeping training sessions short, positive, and fun helps your puppy develop a love for learning. Puppies that have positive training experiences are more likely to stay engaged and excited for future sessions. If training becomes too long or

stressful, your puppy might start to view it as a chore rather than a fun activity. Ending each session on a high note, with a reward and praise, ensures that your puppy remains motivated and eager to continue learning.

- **Preventing Burnout and Frustration**
  Just like people, puppies need rest to avoid burnout. By keeping training sessions short, you reduce the chances of your puppy feeling overwhelmed or stressed. Over time, this leads to a more balanced approach to learning, where your puppy enjoys the process and is excited to participate. Regular breaks between training sessions also give your puppy time to play, relax, and process the information they've learned, which helps them stay focused and ready for the next training opportunity.

Conclusion

Avoiding overtraining is essential to maintaining a positive training experience for both you and your puppy. By recognizing the signs that your puppy is tired or stressed, knowing when to stop a session, and keeping training sessions short and positive, you'll foster an environment where your puppy can learn without feeling overwhelmed. The long-term benefits of brief, focused training sessions include better retention, a stronger bond between you and your puppy, and a more enjoyable learning experience overall. With patience, consistency, and the right approach, you'll be able to set your puppy up for success, both in their training and in their relationship with you.

Using Redirection Instead of Punishment

When you're training your puppy, one of the most important things to remember is that **punishment** isn't the most effective way to shape behavior. In fact, punishment can often backfire, leading to fear, confusion, and a damaged bond between you and your puppy. Instead of focusing on punishing unwanted behaviors, **redirection**—guiding your puppy to more appropriate behaviors—is far more effective and much kinder. In this section, we'll explore why punishment doesn't work, how to redirect unwanted behaviors to more acceptable actions, and the power of reinforcing positive behavior while ignoring undesired actions.

1. Why Punishment Doesn't Work and What to Do Instead

Punishment, whether it's physical correction, yelling, or using negative reinforcement, can create fear and anxiety in puppies, which often leads to confusion and worsens undesirable behaviors. When you punish a puppy, they may not understand exactly why they're being punished or how to fix the behavior, which makes it harder for them to learn. Instead of punishing, we can focus on more effective, compassionate strategies like redirection.

- **Punishment Can Lead to Fear and Anxiety**
  Puppies are still learning about the world and trying to figure out what's expected of them. If you punish them for behaviors you don't like, they may become fearful or anxious, which can result in further behavioral issues. For example, if you yell at your puppy for chewing on shoes, they might associate you with fear and start avoiding you, rather than learning to stop chewing on shoes. This can damage your bond with your puppy and prevent them from trusting you.

- **Punishment Doesn't Teach the Right Behavior**

Punishment doesn't provide your puppy with an alternative behavior. When a puppy is punished for doing something wrong, they may become confused about what they *should* be doing. For example, scolding your puppy for jumping on the furniture doesn't tell them where they *should* be. Instead of focusing on the negative, you want to show your puppy exactly what you want them to do instead. This is where redirection comes in.

- **Redirection Offers Clear Guidance**
  Redirection is a positive approach where you guide your puppy from an unwanted behavior to a more desirable one. This technique works because it teaches the puppy *what to do* instead of just *what not to do.* By offering an alternative behavior, you help your puppy succeed and keep training sessions fun, productive, and stress-free.

2. Redirecting Unwanted Behaviors with Appropriate Alternatives

When your puppy starts engaging in undesirable behaviors, the goal is to gently steer them toward more acceptable actions. Redirection works best when you offer something that your puppy finds rewarding—

whether that's a toy, a different activity, or a command
that they already know. Here's how to redirect effectively:

- **Distract with Toys or Chews**
  If your puppy is chewing on something they
  shouldn't (like your shoes or furniture), give
  them a toy or chew they are allowed to chew on
  instead. The key here is to offer an alternative
  that's just as interesting, if not more interesting,
  than what they're currently doing. For example,
  you might give your puppy a rubber toy filled
  with treats or a sturdy chew bone that keeps
  them engaged.

- **Use Commands to Interrupt the Behavior**
  If your puppy is engaging in an undesired
  behavior like jumping or barking excessively, use
  a command that redirects them to something
  positive. For instance, if your puppy is jumping
  on guests, calmly say "sit" to guide them to a
  more appropriate behavior. When they follow
  your command, reward them with praise or
  treats to reinforce that the alternative behavior is
  what you want.

- **Redirect to Positive Activities**
  Redirecting doesn't always have to involve toys

or commands. Sometimes, you can simply offer your puppy an activity that is more engaging than what they're doing. For example, if your puppy is digging in the garden, take them to a designated digging spot where it's acceptable for them to dig, or engage them in a game of fetch to distract them from the unwanted behavior.

3. The Power of Reinforcing Desired Behaviors and Ignoring Undesired Ones

While redirection is a helpful tool, it's also important to use reinforcement to encourage your puppy to repeat the behaviors you want to see more often. This strategy is all about rewarding good behavior and **ignoring** undesirable behavior whenever possible. The key here is to make the desired behavior the easiest and most rewarding option for your puppy.

- **Reinforce Positive Behaviors Immediately**
  Whenever your puppy does something you like—whether it's sitting calmly, following a command, or playing gently—immediately reward them with praise, treats, or their favorite toy. The quicker you reward, the stronger the connection your puppy will make between the behavior and the reward. For example, if your

puppy sits quietly on the couch, give them a treat and praise them for being calm. This reinforces the behavior you want to see more of.

- **Ignore Undesired Behaviors When Safe to Do So**
  If your puppy is engaging in a behavior you don't like, but it's not harmful or dangerous, try to simply ignore it. Puppies often seek attention by engaging in unwanted behaviors like barking, whining, or jumping. If you respond with attention (even negative attention like scolding), you might inadvertently reinforce the behavior. Instead, turn your back, stay quiet, or walk away until your puppy calms down or redirects their focus. This teaches them that undesired behaviors don't result in attention, but calm behavior does.

- **Use "Catch Them Being Good"**
  One of the most powerful tools for reinforcing positive behavior is the concept of "catching them being good." This means you actively look for moments when your puppy is displaying desirable behavior—whether that's sitting quietly, walking calmly on a leash, or playing gently with a toy. When you notice these

moments, reward them immediately. This not only reinforces those behaviors but also helps shift the focus from correcting bad behavior to rewarding good behavior.

Conclusion

Using redirection instead of punishment is an effective and compassionate way to guide your puppy's behavior. By offering appropriate alternatives and reinforcing the behaviors you want to see more of, you create a positive training environment where your puppy can thrive. Remember, punishment doesn't teach your puppy what to do—it just tells them what not to do. With redirection, you not only help your puppy learn what is expected, but you also strengthen your bond by building trust and creating a positive, enjoyable training experience. By reinforcing good behavior and ignoring unwanted actions, you're setting your puppy up for long-term success and a harmonious relationship.

Chapter 3

Training on the Go: Maximizing Your Busy Schedule

Training While Walking

Walks are one of the best opportunities to bond with your puppy while also reinforcing their training in real-world environments. Whether you're out for a leisurely stroll or navigating a busy street, walks provide an ideal setting to practice basic commands, improve focus, and encourage good behavior. Incorporating training into your walk doesn't have to be time-consuming or complicated—simple adjustments can make walks productive and enjoyable for both you and your puppy. In this section, we'll explore how to use walks as a training opportunity, including practicing commands like "sit" and "heel," reinforcing focus and good behavior in public spaces, and the benefits of leash training.

1. Incorporating Basic Commands Like "Sit" or "Heel" While on Walks

Walks are the perfect time to reinforce basic commands like "sit," "heel," and "stay." These commands aren't just for indoor training—they're essential tools that help your puppy navigate the outside world safely and respectfully. By practicing these commands during walks, you're integrating training into your daily routine without extra effort.

- **Practice "Sit" at Intersections or Stops**
  When you stop at an intersection, traffic light, or before crossing the street, use this moment as an opportunity to practice the "sit" command. This helps your puppy understand the importance of waiting calmly during breaks in the walk and prevents them from pulling or darting out in an uncontrolled way. As soon as your puppy sits, reward them with praise or a treat to reinforce the behavior. This encourages patience and teaches them to focus on you during distractions.

- **Incorporate "Heel" to Improve Leash Etiquette**
  Teaching your puppy to "heel" while walking on

a leash ensures that they stay by your side and don't pull. To reinforce this behavior, every time your puppy starts to pull, gently tug the leash back toward you, and then immediately give the "heel" command. Walk in sync with them and reward them when they are walking calmly at your side. Over time, your puppy will associate walking calmly with positive rewards and will be more likely to stay close to you.

- **Use Walks to Practice "Leave It" and "Wait"**
  Public spaces are full of distractions—other dogs, food scraps, leaves blowing by—but these distractions offer excellent opportunities to practice commands like "leave it" and "wait." If your puppy becomes interested in something undesirable (like a piece of food on the ground), use the "leave it" command and reward them when they obey. Similarly, if you stop to chat with someone or take a break, use the "wait" command to teach them to stay calm and remain in place until you give the cue to move again.

2. Using Walks to Reinforce Focus and Good Behavior in Public Spaces

Walks are one of the best ways to reinforce focus and good behavior, especially when navigating public spaces. The outdoors is full of distractions, and training your puppy to stay focused on you despite these distractions helps build reliability in their training.

- **Reinforce Focus with Frequent Praise**
  As you walk, frequently check in with your puppy to make sure they're paying attention to you. If your puppy looks up at you or stays focused on walking calmly by your side, reward them with praise or a small treat. This helps reinforce the idea that looking to you for guidance is rewarding, especially when there are distractions like other people, dogs, or sounds.

- **Practice Loose Leash Walking**
  Keeping your puppy's attention on you while walking is the cornerstone of loose-leash walking. A puppy that pulls constantly is not paying attention to you, which can make walks stressful. To combat this, when your puppy pulls, stop walking immediately. Wait until the leash is slack, and reward your puppy for

walking calmly at your side. Reinforce this behavior consistently by rewarding them every time they are walking politely. This teaches your puppy that good behavior leads to more enjoyable walks.

- **Use Distractions to Your Advantage**
  Public spaces—parks, sidewalks, and other pet-friendly areas—are full of distractions. These can be used as opportunities to teach your puppy how to stay focused despite external stimuli. Practice commands like "sit," "stay," or "look at me" in the presence of distractions. Gradually increase the level of distraction (such as walking near other dogs or in busier areas) while rewarding your puppy for staying focused. Over time, your puppy will learn to maintain good behavior even when surrounded by distractions.

3. The Benefits of Adding Leash Training to Your Routine to Improve Behavior

Leash training is not just about teaching your puppy how to walk calmly on a leash—it's also about building communication, discipline, and safety. Adding leash training to your routine will help improve your puppy's overall behavior, both on walks and at home.

- **Improved Control and Safety**

  A well-trained puppy on a leash is safer for both of you. Leash training ensures that your puppy doesn't pull toward hazards, such as oncoming traffic, other dogs, or dangerous objects. Having control over your puppy while walking gives you peace of mind, knowing that you can guide them safely through any situation.

- **Strengthened Bond Between You and Your Puppy**

  Training your puppy to walk calmly on a leash strengthens the bond between you and your dog. As you practice commands and reinforce good behavior, you are communicating with your puppy and building trust. Your puppy learns to rely on you for guidance, which improves your overall relationship and makes future training sessions easier and more enjoyable.

- **A More Enjoyable Walking Experience for Both of You**

  Leash training helps reduce the stress that comes from a puppy that constantly pulls, lunges, or gets distracted during walks. When your puppy understands the boundaries of leash walking, both of you can enjoy a calm, peaceful walk. This provides an opportunity for your puppy to get the exercise they need while also reinforcing good behavior and focus. As your puppy becomes more confident on the leash, walks will become a fun and enjoyable activity for both of you to share.

Conclusion

Training while walking is an excellent way to reinforce basic commands, improve leash etiquette, and teach your puppy how to stay focused and well-behaved in public spaces. By incorporating simple commands like "sit" and "heel" into your daily walks, you not only improve your puppy's behavior but also make walks more enjoyable and productive. The benefits of leash training go beyond just teaching your puppy to walk politely—they strengthen the bond between you and your puppy, ensure safety, and help create a calm and enjoyable experience for both of you. With consistent practice, walks can become a valuable part of your puppy's training routine, providing opportunities for growth and connection every time you head out the door.

Training While Traveling or Running Errands

As a busy person, you're likely on the go a lot—whether that's running errands, commuting, or traveling. The good news is that even during these moments of travel and downtime, you can continue to reinforce your puppy's training. Car rides and quick stops at stores or parks provide perfect opportunities to practice commands and keep your puppy mentally engaged. These real-world training scenarios help your puppy adapt to different environments, reinforcing calm behavior and focus in a variety of settings. In this section, we'll explore how to use car rides and errand runs as training opportunities, teach your puppy to stay calm during downtime, and keep them engaged when they need to be patient.

1. How to Use Car Rides or Errands as Chances to Practice Commands

Car rides and short trips are a great time to reinforce commands like "settle," "stay," and "wait." Training your puppy to be calm and well-behaved during car rides or while running errands helps them learn how to manage excitement and anxiety in different environments. These moments can also help your puppy become comfortable with new experiences and prevent car-related stress or restlessness.

- **Practice "Settle" in the Car**

    One of the most useful commands you can teach your puppy for car rides is "settle." Puppies often get excited during car trips, whether they're anticipating a walk or simply because the car is a novel experience. To teach "settle," start by putting your puppy in the car, and once they are in their seat, give the "settle" command. Reward them when they calm down and remain in a relaxed position. Repeat this whenever you're in the car to encourage your puppy to stay calm and stop excessive movement. Over time, your puppy will associate car rides with calm behavior rather than restlessness.

- **Use "Wait" When Stopping at Stores or Parks**

    Errand stops provide great opportunities to teach your puppy the "wait" command. Whether you're popping into a store or stopping at a park, train your puppy to wait calmly before you exit or re-enter the car. To practice, open the door slightly and say "wait" before you allow your puppy to step out. You can then reward them for staying calm and not rushing out of the vehicle. This command also helps your puppy understand boundaries and teaches them patience in situations where there's excitement or anticipation.

- **Reinforce Calmness Before Leaving the Car**
Before getting out of the car, ask your puppy to "sit" or "wait" until you give the cue to get out. This ensures that your puppy isn't bolting out of the car the moment you open the door. This is especially useful for busy areas where you need control over your puppy. Reward your puppy for staying put while you're opening the door or getting out yourself. This teaches them to remain calm and focused until it's time to act.

2. Using Short Stops to Teach Your Puppy to Wait Calmly or Stay in Place

Errand stops or quick pit stops are excellent opportunities to teach your puppy to wait calmly in place, whether that's in the car or at a store. Teaching patience and calmness during these brief pauses in your routine helps to set your puppy up for good behavior in other similar situations.

- **Teach "Stay" at Every Stop**

  Whenever you make a stop, whether it's at a gas station or a store, practice the "stay" command with your puppy. For example, when you arrive at your destination, ask your puppy to "stay" in a spot while you complete your errand. Gradually increase the duration of the stay, rewarding your puppy for remaining in place and quiet. The key is to start with short periods and gradually build up to longer waits as your puppy becomes more comfortable with staying in place.

- **Practice Calm Behavior During Short Waits**

  Use moments when you're waiting in the car or standing in line at the store to practice calmness and patience. If your puppy starts to get antsy or fidgety, gently guide them back to a relaxed position and reinforce the calm behavior. This is a great opportunity to reward them for waiting quietly or for not reacting to external distractions (like other people or dogs). When your puppy learns that staying calm results in rewards, they'll be more likely to settle down in similar situations in the future.

- **Incorporate "Look at Me" to Refocus Your Puppy**

  Sometimes, during these short stops, your puppy may become distracted by new sights, sounds, or smells. To refocus their attention, use the "look at me" command. This encourages your puppy to pay attention to you, which helps reinforce the bond between you and redirects their focus away from distractions. Reward them when they make eye contact and stay focused on you, reinforcing the idea that paying attention to you is a positive behavior.

3. Keeping Your Puppy Engaged with Mental Stimulation During Downtime

Even though you're busy running errands or traveling, you don't want your puppy to become bored or restless. Bored puppies are more likely to engage in undesirable behaviors. By incorporating mental stimulation into your routine, you can keep your puppy engaged and help them use their energy in positive ways, even during downtime.

- **Use Puzzle Toys and Treat Dispensers**

  Puzzle toys are a great way to keep your puppy mentally engaged during car rides or while you're running errands. These toys stimulate your puppy's brain by requiring them to solve simple problems, like figuring out how to release treats. Before you start a car ride or head out for an errand, pack a puzzle toy or a treat-dispensing ball. This helps keep your puppy entertained and focused while also reducing boredom.

- **Short Training Sessions During Breaks**
  If you're taking a short break during a trip or errand run, use the opportunity to do a brief training session with your puppy. Even a few minutes of focused training—like practicing "sit," "stay," or "look at me"—can provide mental stimulation and reinforce good behavior. The key is to keep training sessions short but consistent, as even brief periods of training can provide a mental workout for your puppy.

- **Give Your Puppy a Safe and Comfortable Space**
  Whether you're traveling in the car or waiting in a public space, make sure your puppy has a comfortable, safe place to rest and relax. A well-padded crate or car seat cover can give your puppy a sense of security during downtime, helping them feel calm and settled. A cozy space can also encourage your puppy to rest and stay

out of trouble during long periods of waiting. If you're running errands, consider using a portable crate or car seat cover to create a familiar environment for your puppy to relax in between activities.

Conclusion

Training your puppy while traveling or running errands is a great way to reinforce good behavior, teach patience, and keep them mentally stimulated on the go. Whether it's practicing commands like "settle" during car rides, teaching your puppy to "stay" during short stops, or using mental enrichment activities to pass the time, these moments provide valuable opportunities for training without additional time commitment. By integrating training into your daily routine, you make the most of your busy schedule while setting your puppy up for success in the real world. With consistency and positive reinforcement, these travel and errand-based training sessions will become an enjoyable part of your puppy's education—and yours.

Training During Playtime

Playtime isn't just about fun—it's a fantastic opportunity to reinforce your puppy's training in a relaxed, positive environment. By turning play into a training session, you can teach essential commands while strengthening your bond with your puppy. Playtime also offers a natural setting to reinforce obedience and good behavior, allowing you to incorporate training without it feeling like a chore. In this section, we'll explore how you can use playtime as a productive training tool, practice commands like "drop it" or "fetch," and use toys to encourage positive behavior.

1. Turning Play into a Training Session by Reinforcing Commands like "Drop It" or "Fetch"

One of the best ways to integrate training into playtime is to incorporate commands like "drop it" and "fetch" during games. These commands are not only useful for managing toys but also help reinforce your puppy's obedience in a fun and engaging way. Playtime is ideal for teaching these commands because your puppy is already excited and motivated by the activity.

- **"Drop It" During Play**
  Playtime often involves tugging, chewing, or playing with toys, which makes it the perfect time to teach your puppy the "drop it" command. During a game of tug-of-war or fetch, when your puppy grabs onto the toy, give

the "drop it" command. If your puppy releases the toy, immediately reward them with praise or a treat. If they don't let go, offer a treat or another toy in exchange. The goal is to make "drop it" a positive and rewarding experience. Over time, your puppy will learn that letting go of toys when asked results in more play or treats, making them more likely to obey the command.

- **Using "Fetch" to Practice Recall**
  Fetch is another great game that reinforces obedience, especially the recall command. When your puppy brings the toy back to you, say "come" or "fetch" and reward them when they return the toy. If your puppy doesn't bring the toy back right away, use the "come" command to encourage them. It's important to keep the game fun and rewarding, so they associate coming to you with positive outcomes. Playing fetch is not only great for physical exercise, but it also reinforces recall skills in a low-pressure environment.

- **Reinforcing "Leave It" with Play**
  "Leave it" is an important command, especially when you want your puppy to stop focusing on something they shouldn't be engaging with.

Playtime is an ideal time to reinforce this command. If your puppy picks up something they shouldn't, like a sock or shoe, say "leave it" and then offer them a toy or treat as an alternative. Reward them for obeying, and keep the session light and fun. By practicing "leave it" during play, your puppy will learn to pay attention to you even when they are distracted by other items.

2. Incorporating Games to Strengthen the Bond and Reinforce Obedience

Games are a great way to reinforce obedience in a way that feels fun for both you and your puppy. When you use games to practice commands and focus, you not only teach your puppy important skills but also build a stronger relationship. Playtime can enhance trust, communication, and the bond between you and your puppy, making them more likely to respond positively during formal training sessions.

- **Interactive Games for Bonding**
  Games like tug-of-war, hide-and-seek, and fetch create opportunities for interaction that reinforce your bond. During these games, use commands like "sit" before you start playing,

"stay" while you hide the toy, or "drop it" when you want your puppy to release the toy. By using commands during these games, you show your puppy that following directions doesn't take the fun out of playtime—it actually makes the game more enjoyable. This strengthens your relationship and encourages your puppy to listen to you, as they begin to associate training with positive experiences.

- **Incorporating Training into Tug-of-War**
  Tug-of-war is not only a great way for your puppy to burn off energy but also an opportunity to practice impulse control and obedience. Before starting a tug session, ask your puppy to "sit" and "stay." Once they are in position, begin the game, but stop frequently to practice "drop it" or "take it" to reinforce their response to commands. By stopping the game at intervals to reinforce obedience, your puppy learns that following your commands is part of the game. This helps them develop self-control and reinforces positive behavior.

- **Use Play to Build Trust and Confidence**
  Playtime is one of the best ways to build trust with your puppy, as it's a time for them to

engage with you in a positive, low-stress environment. When you incorporate training into play, you are teaching your puppy to trust that you are in control and that following your cues will lead to rewards. This builds confidence, making them more eager to listen to you during training sessions and in everyday situations. For example, if you play "hide and seek" with treats, your puppy will learn that following your cues and listening to your commands helps them find rewards, which boosts their confidence.

3. Using Toys to Encourage Positive Behavior, Like Sitting Before Play Begins

Using toys during training is a powerful way to reinforce positive behaviors, such as sitting before play or waiting for your cue to start a game. This helps your puppy understand that good behavior leads to playtime and fun, while undesirable behavior (like jumping or rushing) results in a pause. By integrating obedience into play, you teach your puppy to be patient and wait for your signal before engaging in exciting activities.

- **Teach "Sit" Before Play Starts**

  Teaching your puppy to "sit" before starting a game helps reinforce calm behavior and prevents them from jumping or getting overly excited. Before starting playtime, ask your puppy to sit and reward them when they do. Once they are sitting calmly, begin the game. This teaches your puppy that they have to be patient and follow your commands before they get what they want. Over time, this will become a natural habit for them, and they'll be more likely to remain calm and focused when playtime begins.

- **Use Toys to Reinforce Calmness**
  If your puppy starts to get overly excited or jumps while you're preparing to play, pause the game and wait for them to calm down. Once your puppy is sitting or relaxed, reward them with the toy and begin the game. This reinforces the idea that calm, obedient behavior leads to rewards. You can also use a favorite toy to redirect your puppy's focus if they're becoming too hyper. This helps them learn how to control their excitement and focus on the game when appropriate.

- **Incorporate "Stay" and "Leave It" During Play**
  Playtime is an excellent opportunity to teach your puppy to remain in place when you need

them to. Before tossing a ball or toy, use the "stay" command to have your puppy remain still until you give the cue to go. Similarly, if your puppy tries to grab something they shouldn't, use the "leave it" command to redirect their focus to the appropriate toy. This helps your puppy learn to control their impulses and focus on the right behaviors, reinforcing their obedience in a fun, engaging way.

Conclusion

Training during playtime is an excellent way to reinforce key commands, strengthen your bond with your puppy, and keep training light and enjoyable. By turning play into a training session, you can reinforce commands like "drop it," "fetch," and "sit" while also teaching impulse control and patience. Playtime provides the perfect environment to integrate obedience into your puppy's daily routine, making training more effective and enjoyable. With consistency and positive reinforcement, your puppy will learn that following commands leads to more fun, and both of you will enjoy the rewarding experience of training through play.

Involving the Whole Family in Training

Training a puppy isn't just the responsibility of one person—it's a family affair! Involving everyone in the household not only ensures your puppy gets consistent training but also strengthens the bond between your puppy and each family member. When multiple people in the household are on the same page with training, your puppy will learn to follow commands from anyone, which helps reinforce obedience in a variety of situations. In this section, we'll discuss how to get everyone in the household on board with training, assign simple tasks to make the process smoother, and ensure consistency in commands and routines.

1. How to Get Everyone in the Household on Board with Training

One of the key components of successful puppy training is ensuring that everyone in the household understands the importance of consistency and is committed to participating. This means getting buy-in from all family members, whether they are adults or children, and making sure everyone is on the same page when it comes to training goals.

- **Start with a Family Training Meeting**

  Before you start training your puppy, have a family meeting to discuss training goals and strategies. Talk about the importance of consistency in commands, timing, and expectations. Agree on the rules and boundaries you want your puppy to follow and make sure everyone understands their role in the training process. This meeting sets the foundation for successful training and helps everyone understand why they need to follow the same routines and commands.

- **Assign Responsibilities Based on Individual Strengths**

  Training doesn't have to fall on just one person. Depending on the age and abilities of each family member, you can assign different training tasks. For example, one person might be responsible for feeding the puppy and reinforcing basic commands like "sit" during mealtime. Another person could handle walks and practicing leash training. Kids can take on smaller tasks like practicing "sit" or "stay" while playing or during downtime. When everyone has a specific role, training becomes a team effort, and your puppy gets well-rounded, consistent guidance.

- **Explain the Benefits of Involvement**
  Help everyone in the household understand that participating in training is not only beneficial for the puppy but also for the family. When everyone is involved, it becomes easier to manage your puppy's behavior, and the puppy learns to respect and listen to all members of the family. This leads to a more harmonious home environment and prevents issues like confusion or frustration with inconsistent rules. Everyone can see that training is an investment in both the puppy's well-being and the household's peace of mind.

2. Assigning Simple Tasks (e.g., One Person Handles Feeding, Another Handles Walking)

Training your puppy is a daily responsibility, and breaking up the tasks into manageable chunks can make it easier and less overwhelming for everyone. Assigning specific tasks to family members can ensure that training becomes part of everyone's routine and that your puppy gets plenty of opportunities to learn throughout the day.

- **Feeding and Basic Command Reinforcement**
  The person responsible for feeding your puppy can incorporate training into mealtime. For example, before giving your puppy their food, ask them to "sit" and wait. Once they sit calmly, reward them by placing the food bowl down. This reinforces the idea that good behavior (sitting and waiting) results in rewards. Other family members can take turns with this task, so your puppy learns to follow the same routine with everyone involved.

- **Walking and Leash Training**
  Taking the puppy for walks is an excellent opportunity to practice commands like "heel," "sit," or "stay" in a real-world environment. Assigning one person or a rotating group of people to handle walks will ensure that training continues outside the home. If your puppy pulls on the leash, gently stop and ask them to "sit" or "stay" before resuming the walk. This helps to reinforce polite walking behavior. Family members can switch off who walks the puppy, so the puppy learns to respond to commands from everyone, not just one person.

- **Playtime and Reinforcing Commands**

  Playtime is another area where family members can contribute to training. Assign someone to initiate games like fetch or tug-of-war while practicing commands like "sit" or "drop it" during play. This helps your puppy understand that training is part of fun activities, and it allows everyone to take part in reinforcing good behavior. By having everyone involved in play, your puppy learns that obedience is not just for training sessions—it's a part of daily life.

3. Ensuring Everyone Uses the Same Commands and Routines for Consistency

Consistency is one of the most important factors in successful puppy training. When everyone in the household uses the same commands and follows the same routines, your puppy will quickly learn what is expected of them. Inconsistent commands or routines can confuse your puppy and delay their progress. Here's how to ensure everyone stays consistent:

- **Use Consistent Commands Across the Family**

  One of the most important aspects of consistency is using the same language for commands. Decide on clear, simple commands that everyone in the family will use. For example, if one person says "sit," make sure everyone else uses the same word, not variations like "sit down" or "sit now." This helps your puppy understand exactly what you mean and speeds up their learning process. Make a list of key commands (e.g., sit, stay, come, leave it) and share it with everyone in the household to avoid confusion.

- **Follow the Same Routine for Meals, Walks, and Play**
  Dogs thrive on routine. Consistency in when and how training happens will help your puppy feel secure and understand expectations. For example, always feed your puppy at the same time each day, and have the same person or people handle the feeding routine so your puppy can associate it with obedience commands like "sit" or "stay." Similarly, try to stick to the same times for walks and play sessions, reinforcing commands during those activities. By making training part of daily routines, your puppy learns that certain behaviors are expected at specific times.

- **Establish Clear Rules and Boundaries for Everyone**

  In addition to using consistent commands, it's important for the whole family to follow the same rules and boundaries for your puppy's behavior. For example, if one family member allows the puppy to jump on the couch and another does not, it can send confusing messages to your puppy. Make sure everyone agrees on the rules and enforces them consistently. Whether it's not allowing your puppy on the furniture, keeping them out of certain rooms, or requiring them to sit before meals, it's essential that everyone in the household sticks to the same rules. This consistency will help your puppy learn boundaries quickly.

Conclusion

Involving the whole family in puppy training is essential for success. By getting everyone on board, assigning simple tasks, and ensuring consistency in commands and routines, you can create a supportive environment where your puppy can thrive. Training becomes easier and more enjoyable when all family members are aligned with the same goals, and your puppy will benefit from hearing the same commands and experiencing consistent routines.

With teamwork and commitment, your puppy will learn to follow instructions from everyone in the household, leading to a well-behaved and well-adjusted puppy—and a harmonious home for all.

Getting Kids Involved in Training

Training a puppy is not just a responsibility for adults—kids can play a crucial role in shaping a puppy's behavior too! Getting children involved in training not only helps reinforce the commands your puppy is learning, but it also teaches kids valuable lessons about responsibility, patience, and positive reinforcement. In this section, we'll explore simple, age-appropriate ways for children to help with training, how to teach kids to use treats and praise effectively, and the powerful benefits of family bonding during training sessions.

1. Simple, Age-Appropriate Ways for Children to Help with Training

Kids can be an amazing asset when it comes to puppy training, as long as the tasks are tailored to their age and abilities. By assigning age-appropriate training tasks, children will feel empowered to help—and puppies will benefit from the additional practice.

- **Young Kids (Ages 4-7): Basic Commands Like "Sit" and "Stay"**

  For younger children, the focus should be on basic commands and simple training exercises. "Sit" and "stay" are perfect commands for kids to practice with their puppy. Kids can offer a treat as a reward when the puppy successfully sits or stays on command. It's important that children are taught to give clear, simple commands and use a calm voice, helping the puppy understand the expectation. These short, fun sessions can also be used as a bonding activity, with kids being rewarded with positive praise for their participation.

- **Older Kids (Ages 8-12): More Advanced Commands and Activities**

  Older children can take on more responsibility in the training process. They can practice not only the basic commands like "sit," "stay," and "come," but also begin to teach their puppy more advanced skills, such as "leave it" or "drop it." At this age, children can help with leash training or reinforcing recall during playtime. They can also help in maintaining the consistency of training by being responsible for certain routines, like feeding the puppy at regular times and practicing commands before meals. These tasks teach kids not only about training but also about the importance of responsibility and patience.

- **Setting Up Training Games for Kids to Lead**

  Training doesn't always have to be serious—games are a great way to keep kids engaged while reinforcing the puppy's behavior. Kids can lead simple games like "fetch" or "hide and seek" with the puppy, using basic commands throughout the game. For example, before throwing a ball, the child can ask the puppy to "sit" or "stay" as part of the game. Kids learn that obedience is required before the fun starts, and the puppy practices following commands in a playful context.

2. How to Teach Kids to Use Treats and Praise Effectively Without Overwhelming the Puppy

Using treats and praise is one of the most effective ways to reinforce positive behavior, but when it comes to children, it's important to teach them the right way to use rewards without overwhelming the puppy.

- **Start Small: Teach Kids to Use Treats Sparingly**

  Teach kids that treats are rewards for good behavior, but they shouldn't be used too frequently, especially with puppies who are still learning. Kids should give treats only after the puppy follows a command successfully. For example, after a puppy sits on command, the child can reward them with a small treat and praise like "Good boy!" or "Nice job!" It's important that kids understand that treats are used to reinforce good behavior, not as an ongoing indulgence. Encourage them to use small treats or even portions of their regular kibble to avoid overfeeding.

- **Praise First, Then Treats**

  Kids should be taught to immediately praise their puppy when it follows a command. This positive reinforcement helps the puppy understand that they did something right. After praise, they can then offer a treat to further cement the behavior. The praise should come first because it helps create a bond and boosts the puppy's confidence, making them more likely to repeat the behavior. Kids should say things like "Good puppy!" in a happy, enthusiastic voice, which helps the puppy feel rewarded before receiving the treat.

- **Limit the Number of Treats**
  Help kids understand that too many treats can overwhelm the puppy and possibly lead to bad habits, like begging for food. Teach them to use treats intermittently (not after every command) to keep the training fresh and exciting for the puppy. For example, praise and treat the puppy every other time they follow a command, or use a toy as a reward occasionally. This variation in rewards helps the puppy stay engaged and motivated without becoming overly reliant on food.

3. The Benefits of Family Bonding During Training Sessions

Training sessions are a wonderful opportunity for the entire family to come together and bond over a shared activity. When kids participate in training, they not only contribute to the puppy's development but also create lasting memories and a stronger relationship with their pet.

- **Strengthening the Parent-Child-Puppy Relationship**

  Family training sessions offer a way for both parents and children to work together with the puppy. By assigning roles, everyone can feel involved and valued in the training process. For example, parents can oversee the training, while kids can practice specific commands and reward the puppy. This cooperation strengthens the relationship between the puppy and each family member, creating a positive atmosphere where everyone plays an active role in the puppy's learning journey.

- **Teaching Kids Responsibility and Patience**

  One of the greatest benefits of getting kids involved in training is that it teaches them responsibility and patience. Training a puppy requires consistency, time, and effort. When children help train a puppy, they learn that rewards come after hard work, and that some things take time to learn. It also gives them a sense of pride when they see their puppy successfully following a command they've helped teach. This responsibility can carry over to other areas of life, teaching kids valuable life skills such as patience, commitment, and problem-solving.

- **Creating Lasting Memories**
  Training sessions can be a fun family activity that creates lasting memories for everyone involved. Whether it's the first time your child successfully teaches the puppy to sit, or when the whole family celebrates a milestone in the puppy's training progress, these moments build a special bond between your puppy and your kids. As your puppy grows and becomes more obedient, your family will have the satisfaction of knowing that everyone contributed to shaping their behavior, fostering a deeper connection that lasts throughout the puppy's life.

Conclusion

Involving kids in puppy training is a fantastic way to create a positive, family-centered experience. By assigning age-appropriate tasks, teaching kids how to use treats and praise effectively, and making training a fun, shared activity, you're not only helping your puppy learn essential commands but also fostering a strong, loving relationship between your puppy and your children. The lessons learned in training—responsibility, patience, and teamwork—extend far beyond the puppy years, creating lifelong bonds and happy memories for the entire family.

Managing Training in Busy Households

In a busy household, it can feel like there's never enough time to fit everything in—especially when it comes to training a puppy. Between work, school, chores, and other commitments, adding consistent training sessions to the mix might seem overwhelming. However, with a little planning and flexibility, you can incorporate quick, effective training into your daily routine without feeling stressed or rushed. In this section, we'll discuss how to fit in short training sessions during the busiest times of day, create a training routine that works for everyone in the family, and use tools like shared calendars and checklists to stay organized and on track.

1. How to Fit in Quick Training Sessions During the Busiest Times of Day

Even on the busiest days, you can squeeze in short training sessions that are just as effective as longer ones. The key is to recognize those small windows of opportunity when you can engage with your puppy for 5 to 10 minutes. These quick training bursts can be spread throughout the day, keeping your puppy on track without requiring a large time commitment.

- **Before or After Meals**
  Meal times can be an excellent opportunity to work on basic commands like "sit," "stay," or "leave it." Before putting your puppy's food bowl down, ask them to sit and wait calmly. Once they've followed the command, reward them with their food. This routine can become a regular part of mealtimes, and because everyone in the household needs to feed the puppy, it's an easy way to get multiple family members involved in training, even if they have different schedules.

- **During Downtime (e.g., TV Time, Waiting for the Bus)**
  You don't always need to schedule formal training sessions—training can happen during downtime too. For example, while waiting for dinner to cook or watching TV, you can practice commands like "sit," "stay," or "come" with your puppy. These small, informal training sessions are a great way to integrate training into your daily life without feeling like you need to carve out extra time. Even in brief moments,

consistency is key, so you can reinforce behaviors in a relaxed, stress-free environment.

- **While Out on Walks**
  Walks can also double as training opportunities. While you're walking your puppy, you can practice leash walking, reinforce basic commands like "heel," or ask them to sit or stay when you stop. You don't need a separate time or space for this—simply use your walks to reinforce good behavior in real-world situations. This can be especially helpful for busy families on the go since walks are a necessary part of daily life.

2. Creating a Routine That Everyone in the Family Can Follow, Even with Different Schedules

In a busy household, everyone has different schedules, but that doesn't mean puppy training can't be a part of each person's day. The key is to create a flexible training routine that works around your family's unique schedules while ensuring that everyone participates.

- **Set Fixed Training Times**
  One of the easiest ways to keep everyone involved is to set fixed, family-wide training

times that fit into your household's routine. For example, you could designate 5 minutes in the morning to practice "sit" before everyone leaves for work or school, and another 5 minutes in the evening to work on leash training before dinner. Even if the times are short, having these training windows at set times each day can help create consistency and ensure that the puppy gets the attention they need. If a family member is unable to participate at a particular time, they can take over training during another part of the day.

- **Rotate Responsibilities**

  In a busy household, everyone likely has different time commitments, so it's helpful to rotate responsibilities. For example, one person could handle morning training, while another person takes care of the afternoon session. If you have kids, you can assign them simple tasks like practicing "sit" before dinner or before playtime. By rotating tasks, everyone stays involved, and the puppy gets multiple opportunities to learn from different family members, reinforcing consistency in commands and routines.

- **Build Training into Existing Routines**

  Try to weave training into existing routines. For example, if you're getting ready for bed, you can practice "sit" and "stay" as part of winding down. Or, if someone is going out to do errands, they can take the puppy for a short walk and reinforce commands like "heel" or "sit" while out. By linking training to activities your family already does, you won't need to create separate time slots, making it easier to stick to the routine even with a busy schedule.

3. Using a Shared Calendar or Checklist to Keep Everyone Accountable and Involved

A shared calendar or checklist is an excellent tool for keeping track of training sessions, ensuring that everyone is on the same page, and holding each family member accountable. Whether you're coordinating training times, sharing responsibilities, or tracking your puppy's progress, these tools can help make training feel organized and manageable.

- **Shared Calendar for Family Scheduling**

  A shared digital calendar (like Google Calendar or a family scheduling app) can be a lifesaver for coordinating training sessions across different schedules. You can create recurring events or reminders for specific training tasks, such as "10-minute training session" or "puppy walk and practice sit." By adding these reminders to a shared calendar, everyone in the family can see when they are responsible for training, and it's easy to find time slots that work for everyone. Plus, the calendar acts as a visual reminder of your puppy's progress and any areas that may need more attention.

- **Training Checklist for Daily Accountability**
  A simple checklist can be a powerful tool for ensuring that each family member completes their designated training tasks. You can create a checklist of daily or weekly training activities (e.g., practice "sit," work on leash walking, reinforce crate training) and assign tasks to different family members. As tasks are completed, family members can check them off, keeping the process organized and on track. You can also use this checklist to track progress over time, noting improvements and areas where additional focus is needed.

- **Tracking Progress and Goals**
  In addition to using a shared calendar and

checklist, it's also helpful to track your puppy's progress and set training goals. You can keep a simple journal or use a training app to monitor your puppy's development. For example, if your puppy is consistently sitting before meals, you can celebrate that milestone and set a new goal for walking on a leash without pulling. Tracking progress keeps everyone motivated and ensures that training stays consistent and goal-oriented, even during busy times.

Conclusion

Managing puppy training in a busy household is all about maximizing the small windows of time you already have and keeping things simple, consistent, and flexible. By fitting in quick training sessions during the busiest parts of your day, creating a routine that works for everyone in the family, and using tools like shared calendars and checklists to stay organized, you can keep your puppy's training on track without feeling overwhelmed. With a little planning and teamwork, you can make puppy training a seamless part of your busy life, and most importantly, enjoy the process of watching your puppy learn and grow.

Using Treats Wisely

Treats are one of the most effective tools in puppy training, but they need to be used wisely to avoid overfeeding and ensure your puppy stays motivated. The right treats can make training sessions more enjoyable and help reinforce good behaviors, but it's important to choose them carefully, manage their size, and vary them to keep your puppy engaged. In this section, we'll explore how to choose the right treats, manage treat sizes, and use variety to maintain interest during training.

1. How to Choose the Right Treats to Keep Your Puppy Motivated

Choosing the right treats is crucial for keeping your puppy engaged and motivated throughout training. Not all treats are created equal, and selecting the right ones can make a significant difference in your puppy's response to training.

- **Select High-Value Treats for Focused Training**
  High-value treats are those that your puppy finds particularly irresistible. These are especially useful for new or challenging behaviors that require extra motivation. When training new

skills or when your puppy needs extra focus (like during distractions), use treats your puppy truly loves—such as small pieces of chicken, cheese, or a soft, chewy treat. These high-value rewards signal to your puppy that they're doing something particularly good and help keep them motivated when learning something new.

- **Use Healthier Treats for Everyday Training**
  For daily practice and more routine commands, opt for healthy, lower-calorie treats that your puppy enjoys but won't overindulge in. Treats like small bits of carrot, apple, or low-calorie commercial puppy treats can work well for reinforcing basic behaviors. Look for treats that are made with simple ingredients and that suit your puppy's dietary needs, as these are healthier options that won't contribute to weight gain when used regularly.

- **Consider Size and Texture**
  Treats that are too large can be difficult to use during training, especially when you need to give several rewards in a short period. Choose small treats that are easy to break into pieces or soft enough to quickly chew. The texture matters, too—some puppies prefer soft, chewy treats,

while others may prefer crunchy ones. Finding a
treat that fits your puppy's preferences can make
training more enjoyable for them and help keep
their attention.

2. Managing Treat Size to Prevent Overfeeding and Ensure It's a Reward

It's easy to give your puppy too many treats, but
managing their size is essential to avoid overfeeding and
ensure that treats remain a meaningful reward. Treats
should be small enough that your puppy can consume
them quickly but large enough to be rewarding.

- **Use Small, Bite-Sized Treats**
  Treats don't have to be large to be effective. In
  fact, small, bite-sized treats are ideal for training
  sessions. They allow you to give multiple
  rewards in a short period without overloading
  your puppy with calories. For example, you can
  use treats that are about the size of a pea or break
  larger treats into smaller pieces. This ensures that
  your puppy gets rewarded often without the risk
  of overfeeding. Small treats also allow you to
  give a quick reward without interrupting the
  flow of the training session.

- **Account for Treats in Your Puppy's Daily Diet**

  Keep track of how many treats you're giving your puppy during the day and adjust their regular meals accordingly. If you're using treats regularly for training, consider reducing the amount of food you're offering at meal times. This way, you prevent overfeeding and maintain your puppy's health while still making training enjoyable. Treats should be considered part of your puppy's daily intake, not an additional source of food. In general, treats should not make up more than 10% of your puppy's total daily calories.

- **Reward in Proportion to the Task**

  The size of the treat should also correspond to the difficulty of the task. For example, if your puppy successfully performs a simple command like "sit," a small treat may be enough. However, for a more complex behavior like learning to "stay" or coming when distracted, consider using a slightly larger or more delicious treat. This proportional approach helps your puppy understand that more challenging tasks are rewarded more generously, which keeps them motivated to learn.

3. The Benefits of Varying the Types of Treats to Maintain Interest

Just like us, puppies can get bored with the same rewards over time. To keep training sessions fun and engaging, vary the types of treats you use. This not only prevents your puppy from becoming disinterested in training, but it can also help you gauge which treats motivate your puppy the most.

- **Introduce Variety to Keep Training Fresh**
  Changing up the types of treats you offer during training sessions keeps your puppy engaged and excited. Use a mix of different flavors, textures, and treat types to maintain their interest. For example, you might use soft treats one day and crunchy treats the next, or swap between meat-based treats and healthier vegetable options. Introducing variety will keep your puppy excited about training and encourage them to focus on the task at hand.

- **Use Toys or Games as Rewards**
  While treats are effective, toys and games can also be powerful rewards, especially when you

want to add a bit of fun to your training. For example, after your puppy performs a command, reward them with a quick game of fetch, tug-of-war, or a favorite chew toy. Using toys as rewards can help reinforce behavior in a more interactive, stimulating way, which can be especially helpful for high-energy puppies.

- **Leverage Environmental Rewards**
  In addition to treats and toys, consider using environmental rewards. For instance, after successfully completing a command, reward your puppy by letting them explore a new area of the yard or go on an extra walk. The environment can serve as a reward, especially for puppies that love to explore and be active. These rewards help make training feel more dynamic and connected to their everyday world.

Conclusion

Treats are a vital part of the training process, but using them wisely is essential to ensure your puppy stays motivated and healthy. By choosing the right treats, managing their size to prevent overfeeding, and varying the rewards to maintain interest, you can make training a fun, engaging experience for both you and your puppy.

With the right approach, treats will become an effective and enjoyable way to reinforce good behavior while strengthening the bond between you and your puppy.

Using Praise and Affection

While treats are an essential part of training, verbal praise and affection are just as important in reinforcing good behavior and building a strong, trusting bond with your puppy. Puppies thrive on positive interactions, and praise can be a powerful motivator—sometimes even more effective than food rewards. In this section, we'll explore why verbal praise is so important, how to balance it with treats, and the role of affection in creating a positive, trusting relationship with your puppy.

1. Why Verbal Praise Is Just as Effective as Treats in Reinforcing Behavior

Verbal praise is an incredibly powerful tool in dog training, often just as effective as treats in reinforcing good behavior. While treats can act as a tangible reward, verbal praise connects with your puppy's emotional state, providing them with affirmation and encouragement. Puppies are eager to please, and the sound of your enthusiastic voice telling them "Good boy!" or "Yes!" can motivate them just as much as a tasty treat.

- **Building Positive Associations with Praise**

  When you use verbal praise consistently, your puppy begins to associate your words with a job well done. Over time, this positive reinforcement helps your puppy understand that good behavior is not just about getting treats—it's about making you happy. This strengthens the bond between you and your puppy and fosters a sense of confidence in them. For example, a simple "Good girl!" after your puppy sits on command can make them feel proud and reinforce their desire to repeat the behavior.

- **Verbal Praise Can Be Immediate and Free**

  One of the greatest advantages of verbal praise is that it's always available. You don't have to worry about running out of treats or carrying them with you everywhere. Verbal praise can be used in any setting, whether you're at home or out for a walk. Simply saying "Yes!" or "Well done!" immediately after your puppy completes a task helps them make a strong connection between the behavior and the reward, even without food.

- **Verbal Praise Strengthens Communication**
  When you use consistent verbal cues, your puppy learns to respond to the tone and inflection of your voice. This helps improve communication and makes training more effective. For example, if your puppy learns that an excited "Yes!" or a high-pitched "Good girl!" means they've done something right, they'll be more likely to repeat the behavior in the future. The more positive interactions you have with your puppy, the better you both communicate and understand each other.

2. How to Balance Praise with Treats to Keep Your Puppy Motivated

While praise is a powerful tool, balancing it with treats is essential for maintaining your puppy's motivation throughout the training process. Using a mix of verbal praise and treats allows you to reinforce good behavior while preventing your puppy from becoming overly reliant on food rewards. The key is to create a system where praise and treats complement each other, making training rewarding without overusing either method.

- **Start with Treats, Transition to Praise**
  In the early stages of training, treats are an

excellent way to encourage your puppy to learn new commands. However, as your puppy becomes more proficient, gradually transition from using treats for every successful command to offering verbal praise and affection more frequently. This helps prevent your puppy from becoming dependent on treats and teaches them that their efforts are valued even without food rewards. For example, after a few successful repetitions of "sit," you might offer praise and a small treat, then continue with just praise for subsequent sits. This gradual shift helps your puppy internalize the behavior and encourages them to perform for the positive feedback rather than always expecting a treat.

- **Use Praise as a Reward for Quick Successes**
  For small, quick successes (like a puppy immediately responding to a basic command), verbal praise alone can be highly motivating. The faster and more frequently you can provide praise, the more likely your puppy will learn to associate positive behavior with your approval. For example, if your puppy immediately sits when you ask, reward them with an enthusiastic "Good boy!" and a pat on the head. Over time,

this keeps the training session fun, with a balance of both verbal praise and occasional treats.

- **Switch Between Praise and Treats to Avoid Complacency**
  To keep your puppy engaged and interested in training, it's important to vary how you reward them. If you always rely on treats, they may start to expect food every time, and their motivation could diminish over time. Switching between praise, affection, and treats keeps your puppy guessing and motivated to perform. For example, after a successful "sit," you might offer a treat and follow up with a gentle scratch behind the ears, or alternate between a few treats followed by several instances of praise alone. This keeps the experience fresh and prevents your puppy from losing interest in training sessions.

3. The Importance of Showing Affection and Building Trust Through Positive Interactions

Affection is a crucial part of training, as it strengthens the emotional bond between you and your puppy. While treats and praise can guide your puppy's behavior, affection is what creates a sense of security and trust, which is essential for a well-adjusted puppy. Puppies need to feel loved, safe, and secure in their environment to learn effectively. Positive interactions help build a foundation of trust that will make training smoother and more enjoyable.

- **Affection Creates a Sense of Security**
  When you show your puppy affection—through petting, cuddling, or gentle words—it reinforces the bond between you and your pet. A puppy that feels safe and loved is more likely to be confident, relaxed, and responsive during training. Affection reassures your puppy that they are doing the right thing, making them more eager to please you. When training feels like a positive, enjoyable experience, your puppy is more likely to remain focused and willing to learn.

- **Positive Interactions Foster a Healthy Relationship**
  Training shouldn't just be about commands and rules—it's an opportunity to deepen your relationship with your puppy. By mixing praise with affection, you create a dynamic where training feels like a shared experience, not a task.

You can show affection during breaks or after a successful session by giving your puppy a cuddle or offering a gentle belly rub. This helps your puppy associate training with positive feelings, making them look forward to future sessions.

- **Affection as a Motivator**

  Affection can also serve as an important motivator. For many puppies, physical affection is just as rewarding as food. If your puppy loves being petted or receiving attention, incorporating affection into training can increase their motivation. For example, after your puppy successfully completes a command, reward them with a few seconds of petting or a favorite scratching spot. The emotional connection you build through these interactions reinforces their desire to continue learning and performing well.

Conclusion

Incorporating praise and affection into your puppy's training routine is just as important as using treats. Verbal praise helps reinforce good behavior, creates positive associations, and strengthens communication between you and your puppy. Balancing praise with treats prevents over-reliance on food rewards and keeps your puppy motivated, while affection fosters trust, security, and a deep emotional bond. By combining these elements in a balanced way, you'll create a training experience that is not only effective but also rewarding and enjoyable for both you and your puppy.

Rewarding Calm Behavior

One of the most valuable skills you can teach your puppy is how to remain calm and relaxed in various situations. While high-energy moments are common in puppyhood, learning to settle down is essential for a well-behaved and happy dog. Teaching your puppy to remain calm and rewarding them for doing so is a key part of their development and training. In this section, we'll explore how to encourage calmness, how to reinforce quiet behavior, and how to use relaxation as a reward throughout the day.

1. Teaching Your Puppy to Remain Calm and Settle in Their Crate or Bed

Teaching your puppy to remain calm and relaxed in their crate or designated bed is a crucial aspect of their training. This helps establish routines, provides them with a safe space, and ensures that they understand when it's time to rest. A calm puppy is easier to manage and will have fewer behavioral problems in the long term.

- **Creating a Positive Crate Association**
  Start by making the crate or bed a positive, comfortable space where your puppy feels safe. Use treats, toys, and affection to encourage your puppy to explore their crate, rewarding them for settling inside. This should not be used as a form of punishment but as a place of relaxation. Place a soft blanket or bed inside, and make sure your puppy has enough room to comfortably stand, lie down, and turn around. Gradually increase the time they spend in the crate or bed, rewarding calm behavior with treats or praise. For example, after your puppy spends a few minutes calmly lying down in the crate, reward them with a treat or gentle petting.

- **Teaching the "Go to Bed" Command**
  A useful command for teaching calmness is the "go to bed" cue. Start by leading your puppy to their crate or designated spot and using a cue word like "bed" or "place." Once your puppy settles down quietly, reward them with praise or a treat. Over time, your puppy will begin to associate the crate or bed with calmness and rest,

making it easier for them to settle down when you need them to. Practice this routine regularly, gradually increasing the duration your puppy stays in the crate or bed, while reinforcing calm behavior.

- **Avoid Overstimulation Before Rest Time**
  Puppies are naturally energetic, so try to avoid stimulating activities right before rest time, as they may have trouble settling down. Instead, wind down with calm activities like gentle petting, a quiet walk, or just relaxing together in the same room. This helps your puppy understand that it's time for rest, not play, and sets the stage for them to settle peacefully in their bed or crate.

2. How to Reinforce Calmness and Quietness as a Form of Positive Behavior

Reinforcing calmness and quietness is just as important as reinforcing active commands like "sit" or "stay." Puppies that learn to settle and remain calm in various situations develop better self-control and are less likely to engage in undesirable behaviors, such as excessive barking, jumping, or destructive chewing.

- **Reward Quiet Moments with Praise or Treats**

  The key to reinforcing calmness is to catch your puppy in the act of being calm and quiet. When your puppy is lying down quietly or just resting peacefully, reward them with verbal praise or a treat. For instance, if your puppy settles quietly while you're eating dinner, calmly say "Good girl" and offer a small treat or affection. This teaches your puppy that calm, quiet behavior is just as rewarding as active behaviors like play or training commands. By rewarding these moments, you help your puppy associate calmness with positive outcomes.

- **Redirect Unwanted Behavior**

  If your puppy starts to become overly excited or is engaging in unwanted behavior (like barking, whining, or jumping), redirect their attention by guiding them to a calm position, like sitting or lying down. Once they settle, immediately reward the calm behavior. It's important not to reward excited or disruptive behavior, as this could reinforce those actions. Instead, redirect your puppy to a more appropriate activity (such as sitting or lying on their bed) and reward them when they achieve calmness.

- **Use "Quiet" as a Cue**

  If your puppy is prone to barking or whining, introduce a "quiet" cue as part of their training. When they start barking or making noise, calmly say "quiet" in a firm, neutral tone, and wait for them to stop. The moment they stop barking, reward them with praise or a treat. Repeat this process consistently so your puppy learns to associate the "quiet" cue with calmness and relaxation. Over time, they'll begin to recognize when it's time to settle down and become quiet.

3. Using Relaxation as a Reward for Good Behavior Throughout the Day

Calmness is not only a learned behavior—it's also an important reward in itself. Puppies need to learn that relaxation and downtime are just as valuable as play or training. Using periods of rest as a reward for good behavior encourages your puppy to see relaxation as a desirable outcome, especially after more active training or play sessions.

- **Calm Playtime as a Reward**

  After a successful training session or a period of

good behavior, reward your puppy with some quiet, relaxing time together. Instead of immediately jumping into a high-energy play session, let your puppy enjoy some downtime with you. Sit together on the couch, give them a gentle belly rub, or let them chew on a favorite toy while you relax nearby. This helps your puppy understand that good behavior and calmness lead to positive experiences, not just playtime or treats.

- **Scheduled Rest Periods**
  Puppies need regular rest, so incorporating short, scheduled breaks throughout the day can help them learn when it's time to relax. After active play or training, give your puppy time to rest in their crate or bed. Use this time as a reward for good behavior—after a successful walk or training session, guide them to their bed for a quiet time. This teaches them that rest is a rewarding part of the routine, not a punishment.

- **Creating Calm Rituals**
  Creating calming rituals throughout the day, such as a quiet cuddle before bedtime or a calm, low-energy walk in the evening, can help reinforce relaxation as a reward. By making calm,

soothing experiences a regular part of your puppy's day, they learn to associate relaxation with positive feelings and reward. For example, you can end your training sessions with a calm, peaceful moment, like letting your puppy sit with you while you pet them softly. This gives your puppy an opportunity to wind down and shows them that relaxation is its own form of reward.

Conclusion

Rewarding calm behavior is a vital part of raising a well-behaved, balanced puppy. By teaching your puppy to remain calm and settle in their crate or bed, you create a foundation of relaxation that will benefit both of you. Reinforcing calmness with praise, treats, and affection ensures that your puppy understands the value of quiet, restful behavior. Using relaxation itself as a reward will help your puppy learn to enjoy downtime and see it as an essential part of their routine. With patience and consistency, your puppy will grow into a calm, well-adjusted companion who knows when it's time to play—and when it's time to rest.

If you are enjoying this book, please spend a few minutes to leave a review on Amazon. This means a lot to me since I am a self-published author and every review makes a big difference.

I also have a Puppy Puzzles (5 simple games to play) thank you gift if you join my mailing list for future book info and announcements. Thank you for your time!

Scan code below with mobile device:

Amazon Review

Puppy Puzzles Gift

Now, let's get back to the training!

Chapter 4

Troubleshooting and Maintaining Long-Term Success

Overcoming Distractions

Training your puppy to focus in distracting environments is an important part of their development, especially as they become more accustomed to the outside world. Whether you're at the park, walking through the neighborhood, or encountering other dogs, it's essential that your puppy learns how to stay focused and calm despite the distractions around them. In this section, we'll explore how to train your puppy to focus amidst distractions, the role of controlled exposure, and how gradual experiences help your puppy build confidence and self-control.

1. How to Train Your Puppy to Focus in Distracting Environments

Puppies are naturally curious and easily distracted, especially when there are new sights, sounds, and smells to explore. Training your puppy to focus on you, even in the most distracting environments, is a valuable skill that will improve their behavior in public spaces and keep them safe. Here's how to help them stay focused:

- **Use High-Value Treats for Motivation**
  In distracting environments, your puppy will need extra motivation to stay focused on you. Bring high-value treats (such as pieces of chicken, cheese, or other puppy favorites) that are more enticing than the distractions around them. When your puppy makes eye contact or listens to your command in a distracting environment, reward them with a high-value treat. Over time, your puppy will begin to associate paying attention to you with receiving something special, making them more likely to focus in future situations.

- **The "Watch Me" Command**
  Teaching your puppy the "watch me" command (or "look") is an excellent way to redirect their

attention when they're distracted. Start by holding a treat near your face and saying "Watch me" or "Look." When your puppy makes eye contact, reward them with the treat and praise. Practice this in quieter environments first, and gradually add distractions (like people, other dogs, or traffic) as your puppy becomes more reliable. This technique helps refocus your puppy's attention on you when their mind is wandering.

- **Gradual Exposure to Distractions**
  Begin training in a calm environment and then gradually introduce distractions. If you're at the park, for instance, start by practicing focus when your puppy is far away from other dogs or people. As your puppy gets better at focusing on you, move closer to the distractions, gradually increasing the difficulty level. This slow progression allows your puppy to learn how to handle distractions without becoming overwhelmed.

2. Using Controlled Distractions to Teach Your Puppy to Remain Calm and Focused

Controlled distractions are an effective way to teach your puppy how to remain calm and focused in different environments. By gradually exposing your puppy to distractions in a controlled way, you can help them develop the self-control needed to ignore temptations and stay engaged with you during training.

- **Simulating Distractions in a Safe Environment**
  Start by simulating distractions in a controlled environment, such as your backyard or living room. For example, you can have a friend walk by with another dog while you practice commands with your puppy. At first, keep the distractions at a low level—this might mean a friend simply walking by or standing in the distance. Reward your puppy when they remain focused and calm during these distractions. Gradually increase the intensity of the distractions, such as having people or other dogs closer by, while continuing to reinforce calm, focused behavior.

- **Incorporating Everyday Distractions**
  Everyday situations can also serve as controlled distractions. For example, you can practice focus while cooking dinner, watching TV, or having visitors over. These types of real-world distractions will help your puppy become accustomed to ignoring everyday stimuli, allowing them to learn how to stay calm and focused even when life is bustling around them. Use treats and praise when your puppy remains calm and focused on you, and gently redirect their attention if they become distracted.

- **The "Leave It" Command**
  The "leave it" command is particularly useful when training your puppy to ignore distractions. Whether it's a toy, food, or another dog, the "leave it" command helps your puppy learn to focus on you rather than reacting impulsively. Start training in a low-distraction environment by placing a treat on the floor and saying "leave it" as your puppy approaches. When they back away from the treat, reward them with a different treat and praise. Gradually increase the difficulty by introducing more tempting

distractions and rewarding calm, focused behavior.

3. The Importance of Gradual Exposure to New Experiences to Build Confidence

One of the most effective ways to help your puppy overcome distractions is by gradually exposing them to new experiences. Just like socialization helps your puppy become accustomed to new people and environments, gradual exposure to distractions builds confidence and teaches your puppy how to cope with them in a calm manner.

- **Start Small and Build Up**
  Begin with less overwhelming distractions and gradually work your way up to more challenging situations. For instance, if your puppy is nervous around other dogs, start by observing other dogs from a distance where your puppy feels safe. Over time, as your puppy becomes more comfortable, you can decrease the distance and eventually practice near dogs during training sessions. This gradual exposure helps your puppy build confidence and reinforces the idea that new experiences can be positive and manageable.

- **Expose to Different Environments**

  Take your puppy to a variety of environments where distractions are likely to occur. This might include places like the park, pet stores, busy sidewalks, or even just a friend's house. Each new experience teaches your puppy how to handle different types of stimuli, and the more experiences they have, the more confident and focused they will become. Reward your puppy for calm behavior in these new environments and increase the difficulty of the distractions over time as your puppy gains confidence.

- **Desensitization Through Repetition**

  Repetition is key when it comes to desensitizing your puppy to distractions. The more your puppy is exposed to various environments and distractions, the more familiar and manageable these situations will become. This process helps reduce anxiety and teaches your puppy how to stay focused and calm even when surrounded by exciting or overwhelming stimuli. Consistently practicing in different locations, with various levels of distractions, will strengthen your puppy's ability to focus in real-world situations.

Conclusion

Overcoming distractions is an important skill for any puppy, as it ensures they stay focused and well-behaved in public spaces, during walks, and in other stimulating environments. By training your puppy to focus using techniques like "watch me," controlled distractions, and gradual exposure to new experiences, you help build their confidence and teach them how to remain calm in challenging situations. With time, patience, and consistent practice, your puppy will learn to focus, stay calm, and respond to commands even when distractions are all around. The key is to make the training process gradual, rewarding calm behavior, and increasing the difficulty of distractions only when your puppy is ready. With this approach, your puppy will grow into a well-adjusted dog who can handle the hustle and bustle of the world with calm composure.

Dealing with Setbacks

Training a puppy is an exciting and rewarding journey, but it's not without its challenges. As with any new skill, setbacks and moments of regression are a natural part of the process. Whether your puppy suddenly forgets a previously learned command, seems less focused, or struggles with consistency, it's important to stay patient and adjust your approach when needed. In this section, we'll discuss how to handle setbacks in training, recognize when a method isn't working, and maintain a positive outlook even when progress feels slow.

1. How to Address Regression in Behavior or Inconsistent Progress

Regression—when your puppy seems to forget previously learned behaviors or begins to exhibit undesirable actions again—is a common part of the training process. It can happen for various reasons, such as changes in routine, new distractions, or developmental stages your puppy is going through. It's important not to get discouraged during these phases.

- **Recognize That Regression is Normal**
  Puppies, like children, go through developmental phases, and they may regress in behavior from time to time. It could be because they are adjusting to new experiences, such as increased socialization, a change in their environment, or even a growth spurt. When this happens, take a step back and remind yourself that this is temporary and part of the learning curve. Puppies often take a few steps forward and then a few steps back before they settle into

new behaviors. The key is consistency in your response.

- **Revisit Basic Commands**

  If your puppy starts regressing or showing inconsistent progress, return to basics. Revisit fundamental commands like "sit," "stay," and "come" to reinforce those foundational behaviors. Keep the sessions short and positive, ensuring that your puppy doesn't feel overwhelmed. This helps your puppy regain confidence in their ability to follow commands, which can help restore their overall focus and motivation. Often, a simple reminder of the basics will help reset your training progress.

- **Be Patient and Don't Punish**

  When setbacks occur, avoid the temptation to punish your puppy for misbehavior. Puppies thrive on positive reinforcement, and harsh reactions can create confusion and anxiety, which will only slow progress. Instead, remain patient and keep your tone calm and consistent. Take breaks when needed and approach training with a relaxed mindset. The more you stay calm and patient, the better your puppy will feel about training and learning in the future.

2. Recognizing When a Training Approach Isn't Working and Trying a New Method

Sometimes, despite your best efforts, a particular training technique or approach may not be producing the desired results. It's important to recognize when a method isn't working and be willing to try something different. Adapting your training style to suit your puppy's unique personality and needs can make a big difference in their progress.

- **Assess the Situation Objectively**
  If your puppy is consistently struggling with a particular command or behavior, it's time to take a step back and evaluate the training method you're using. Ask yourself a few questions:

  - Is my puppy fully understanding what's being asked of them?

  - Are there too many distractions or is the environment overwhelming?

  - Am I using an appropriate amount of reinforcement for the behavior?
    By being honest about whether the current approach is effective, you can

determine if it's time to modify the method or introduce new techniques.

- **Switch Up the Reinforcement**
  If your puppy isn't responding to treats, try switching to a different type of reward, such as playtime, toys, or praise. Some puppies may respond better to different types of reinforcement depending on their personality. For example, a high-energy puppy might be more motivated by a game of fetch than a food treat, while a more food-driven puppy may need higher-value treats. Experimenting with different rewards can help keep your puppy engaged and make training more enjoyable for both of you.

- **Adjust the Difficulty Level**
  If your puppy is struggling with a particular command, try breaking it down into smaller, more manageable steps. Training should be fun and achievable, so don't rush your puppy. If necessary, revisit easier steps that build the foundation for the more complex behavior you're working on. For example, if your puppy isn't getting the "stay" command, try starting with very short durations and gradually increase

the time and distance as they become more confident. Patience and slow progression are often the key to overcoming difficulties.

3. Staying Patient and Keeping a Positive Outlook Even When Things Aren't Perfect

Training a puppy is a long-term commitment, and it's normal to experience ups and downs along the way. When setbacks occur, it's easy to feel frustrated or discouraged, but keeping a positive attitude is essential for both you and your puppy's success. A calm, patient approach will encourage your puppy to stay engaged and motivated to continue learning.

- **Celebrate Small Wins**
  Even if your puppy is struggling with certain behaviors, take time to celebrate the small victories. Every time your puppy succeeds in a training session—whether it's sitting for a few seconds, walking calmly on a leash, or following a new command—it's a step forward. Celebrate these moments with praise and treats to reinforce their progress. Recognizing the little achievements will help maintain your enthusiasm and your puppy's motivation to keep improving.

- **Practice Self-Compassion**
  Remember that training a puppy is a process that requires time and patience. Just as your puppy is learning, so are you. If things aren't going perfectly, don't beat yourself up. Take breaks when necessary, and remind yourself that you are doing your best. It's completely normal to encounter challenges along the way. Self-compassion will help you stay relaxed and positive, creating a supportive environment for both you and your puppy to grow together.

- **Keep a Long-Term Perspective**
  Training a puppy isn't about perfection—it's about progress. Keep a long-term perspective in mind and remember that setbacks are temporary. Puppies are constantly growing and learning, and the skills they gain early on will benefit them throughout their lives. If you stay committed, consistent, and patient, you will see the results of your hard work. The goal is not to achieve perfection, but to build a trusting, respectful bond with your puppy through positive training experiences.

Conclusion

Dealing with setbacks is an inevitable part of training a puppy, but with the right mindset, they can be overcome. Regression and inconsistent progress are normal, and they don't mean you're failing. By remaining patient, assessing your training methods, and being willing to adapt, you can help your puppy get back on track. Remember to celebrate small wins, keep a positive attitude, and focus on progress rather than perfection. Training your puppy is a journey, and every challenge you face is an opportunity to grow together. Stay calm, stay consistent, and trust that, with time, your puppy will continue to develop into a well-behaved and confident companion.

Managing Behavior Issues (e.g., Chewing, Barking)

Every puppy goes through a phase where certain behaviors—like chewing on furniture or incessant barking—can become frustrating for their owners. These behaviors are normal and often stem from a puppy's natural instincts or a lack of proper outlets for their energy. However, with the right training techniques and a little patience, you can manage and redirect these behaviors to create a calmer, more balanced environment for both you and your puppy. In this section, we'll explore how to handle common behavior issues such as chewing and barking, as well as how to use safe spaces and redirection strategies to manage unwanted behaviors.

1. How to Redirect Destructive Behavior with Appropriate Toys and Commands

Puppies explore the world with their mouths, and chewing is a natural way for them to relieve stress, soothe teething discomfort, and satisfy their curiosity. However, when they start chewing on inappropriate items like shoes, furniture, or electrical cords, it can become a problem. Redirecting your puppy's chewing behavior to more appropriate items is key to managing this issue.

- **Provide a Variety of Safe Chew Toys**
  Offer a range of chew toys that are specifically designed for puppies. The more options your puppy has, the less likely they are to chew on your belongings. Look for durable toys that are safe for their teeth, such as rubber or nylon chews, and consider toys that can be stuffed with treats or peanut butter for added interest. You can also rotate the toys regularly to keep them exciting and prevent boredom.

- **Use Commands to Redirect Attention**
  When you catch your puppy in the act of chewing something they shouldn't, calmly say "no" or "leave it," then immediately offer them an appropriate chew toy. When they start chewing the toy, praise them and offer a treat as a reward. This teaches your puppy that chewing on the toy is desirable, while chewing on other items leads to no rewards. Be consistent with the command and redirect as soon as you see them chewing something inappropriate.

- **Prevent Access to Tempting Items**
  Prevention is key when it comes to chewing. When you're not actively supervising your puppy, keep valuable or dangerous items out of their reach. Puppy-proof your home by removing shoes, electrical cords, and household plants that could be harmful. You can also use baby gates or crate training to limit access to certain areas of your home when you're not around to supervise.

2. Teaching Your Puppy to Be Quiet or Settle During Barking Episodes

Excessive barking can be a common challenge for puppy owners, especially when they're excited, anxious, or seeking attention. While it's natural for puppies to bark occasionally, it's important to teach them when it's appropriate to be quiet and settle down.

- **Use the "Quiet" Command**
  Teaching your puppy the "quiet" command can help you manage barking. When your puppy starts barking, calmly say "quiet" in a firm but gentle tone. Wait for them to stop barking (even just for a second) and then reward them with praise or a treat. By rewarding silence, you reinforce the behavior you want. Consistently repeat this during barking episodes to help your puppy learn that being quiet is the behavior that earns rewards.

- **Teach a "Settle" Command**
  In addition to teaching "quiet," you can teach your puppy to settle down when they're feeling overly excited or vocal. Start by saying "settle" and guiding your puppy to a designated resting spot, like their bed or crate. Once your puppy is

in a calm state, reward them with praise or treats. Practice this regularly so your puppy associates the "settle" command with a relaxing, calm behavior. This can be especially useful during high-energy moments like playtime or when you have visitors.

- **Address Barking Triggers**

  Understand what triggers your puppy's barking. Is it excitement, fear, boredom, or attention-seeking? Once you identify the cause, you can address it with specific strategies. For example, if your puppy barks excessively when you leave the house, you may need to gradually desensitize them to departures by practicing short, calm separations. If the barking is due to boredom, increase the amount of mental and physical exercise they get during the day.

3. Using Crates and Safe Spaces to Prevent Unwanted Behaviors When Unsupervised

Crate training and the use of safe spaces are highly effective tools for preventing undesirable behaviors, especially when you're not able to supervise your puppy directly. By providing a safe and controlled environment, you can manage destructive behaviors like chewing and reduce the likelihood of accidents when you're away.

- **The Benefits of Crate Training for Prevention**

  Crates offer a secure space where your puppy can feel safe and comfortable when you're not around to supervise them. Most puppies will naturally avoid soiling their crate or chewing on inappropriate items when confined to a well-sized crate with appropriate toys. Crate training helps prevent destructive behaviors and provides your puppy with a cozy den-like environment that they can retreat to for rest.

- **Create a Puppy-Proofed Safe Area**

  If you don't want to use a crate for long periods, consider setting up a puppy-proofed safe space in your home. This can be a designated room or area, enclosed with gates or a playpen, where your puppy can roam safely. Within this space, ensure that the area is free from hazards, such as valuable or dangerous items, and provide a bed, water, toys, and chew items to keep them entertained and calm. This can be a great solution for preventing unwanted behaviors when you're unable to supervise.

- **Using Safe Spaces to Manage Overstimulation**

   Sometimes puppies can become overstimulated or overly excited, which can lead to unwanted behaviors like chewing or barking. A safe space, such as a crate or quiet room, allows your puppy to calm down and relax in a controlled environment. You can use these safe spaces as a "timeout" when your puppy becomes too worked up. Keep in mind that the crate or playpen should always be associated with positive experiences—never as a form of punishment. This helps ensure that your puppy feels comfortable and safe in their space.

Conclusion

Managing common puppy behavior issues like chewing and barking can be challenging, but with the right strategies, you can teach your puppy better alternatives and prevent unwanted behaviors. By redirecting chewing to appropriate toys, using commands to teach your puppy to be quiet or settle, and utilizing crates or safe spaces when unsupervised, you can create a more peaceful and controlled environment for both you and your puppy. Remember, consistency and positive reinforcement are key, and with patience and persistence, you'll see your puppy develop into a well-behaved companion.

Maintaining a 10-Minute Daily Routine

As a busy pet parent, it's essential to keep puppy training simple, consistent, and manageable. The beauty of a 10-minute daily training routine is that it allows you to achieve long-term success without overwhelming yourself or your puppy. Training in short, focused sessions can help your puppy grow into a well-behaved adult dog while also fitting seamlessly into your busy schedule. In this section, we'll explore how to continue with effective training as your puppy grows, how to adjust your goals, and how to incorporate mental stimulation through games and puzzle toys to keep your puppy engaged.

1. How to Maintain Short, Effective Training Sessions Even as Your Puppy Grows

As your puppy matures, their attention span and learning capacity will evolve. Keeping training sessions short, fun, and effective is key to continued progress and avoiding overwhelm for both of you.

- **Adapt to Your Puppy's Attention Span**
  In the early stages of training, puppies have a

limited attention span, typically around 5 to 10 minutes. As your puppy grows, they may be able to focus for slightly longer sessions, but it's still important to stick to short intervals of focused training. Puppies learn best when the training is broken down into bite-sized pieces. If your puppy starts to lose interest or becomes distracted, it's a sign to end the session on a positive note and come back to it later.

- **Keep Sessions Fun and Engaging**
  A key component of short training sessions is keeping them enjoyable for both you and your puppy. Use positive reinforcement—treats, praise, and play—to motivate your puppy and make training something they look forward to. Mix up the commands and activities to keep things fresh. Even as your puppy grows and learns more complex behaviors, maintain a playful, rewarding atmosphere to ensure they stay engaged and eager to participate.

- **Consistency Over Duration**
  Rather than focusing on the length of each session, prioritize consistency. Regular, brief sessions (even just 10 minutes a day) will have a far greater impact than occasional long sessions.

Establishing a daily routine reinforces good behavior and helps your puppy retain what they've learned. Consistency helps build habits that stick, and as your puppy matures, they'll be more likely to behave without needing constant reminders.

2. Adjusting Training Goals as Your Puppy Masters the Basics and Moves to Advanced Skills

Once your puppy has mastered the basic commands, you'll want to begin challenging them with more advanced skills. Adjusting your training goals ensures you're both progressing and gives your puppy new challenges to conquer.

- **Progress From Basic to Advanced Commands**
  In the early stages of training, you'll focus on foundational commands like "sit," "stay," and "come." As your puppy masters these basics, it's time to introduce more advanced commands and behaviors. For example, you can work on "down," "leave it," or "heel." Gradually introduce new skills that build on the basics, keeping in mind that each new command should be taught in short, clear sessions. The 10-minute training

214

rule still applies, but the complexity of the tasks will increase as your puppy's abilities grow.

- **Introduce Real-World Applications**
  Once your puppy has a good grasp of the basics, you can start introducing training that applies to real-world situations. For example, practicing loose-leash walking during a walk, teaching your puppy to wait calmly in the car, or working on "settle" in distracting environments. This helps your puppy generalize their commands, meaning they can respond in any environment, not just during training sessions at home. Keep these training moments short but consistent, and incorporate them into your daily routine, so your puppy gets plenty of practice in different settings.

- **Maintain Flexibility in Training Goals**
  As your puppy continues to grow, your training goals should evolve based on their temperament, energy levels, and learning pace. Some puppies might quickly pick up complex skills, while others may need more time with basics before progressing. Be flexible and adjust your expectations accordingly. If your puppy is struggling with a new skill, return to simpler

exercises and build back up slowly. Short, 10-minute sessions will help you both stay motivated and ensure your puppy doesn't feel overwhelmed by challenging tasks.

3. Scheduling Time for Mental Stimulation Through Games and Puzzle Toys

Training isn't the only way to provide mental stimulation for your puppy. Incorporating interactive games and puzzle toys into your daily routine can be a fun and effective way to keep your puppy's mind sharp, even on days when you can't dedicate time to formal training.

- **Incorporate Puzzle Toys During Downtime**
  Puzzle toys are an excellent way to keep your puppy mentally engaged while giving them a break from structured training. Toys that require your puppy to solve problems to access treats can provide hours of mental stimulation. These toys help prevent boredom and redirect energy in a productive way. Use them during times when you're busy (e.g., when you're cooking dinner or working from home) to keep your puppy entertained and occupied.

- **Play Games That Reinforce Training**
  Games like hide-and-seek or fetch can also

reinforce training concepts while providing mental exercise. For example, you can hide your puppy's favorite toy or a treat in a safe space and use the "find it" command to encourage them to search. This game builds focus and reinforces obedience in a fun, interactive way. Fetch is another great option, as it encourages your puppy to practice recall ("come") and stay engaged in physical activity.

- **Rotate Activities to Keep Things Fresh**
  Just like with training sessions, keeping things fresh and exciting is important. Avoid letting your puppy get bored with the same games and toys every day. Rotate puzzle toys, games, and activities to keep their mind stimulated and motivated. Even during training sessions, mix up commands, locations, and rewards to keep things interesting. This variation prevents mental burnout and keeps your puppy excited to participate in training and playtime.

Conclusion

Maintaining a 10-minute daily training routine is a manageable and effective way to ensure your puppy continues to learn and grow, even as they become more advanced in their skills. By keeping training sessions short, engaging, and consistent, you'll help your puppy build a solid foundation of good behavior. As they progress, you can adjust your training goals and introduce more complex skills, ensuring that the challenges remain appropriate for their level. Additionally, incorporating mental stimulation through puzzle toys and games will keep your puppy mentally sharp and entertained, reducing the risk of boredom and destructive behaviors. Stick to your routine, be flexible with your goals, and keep training fun and rewarding for both you and your puppy.

Continuing Socialization

Socialization is one of the most important aspects of puppy training. The experiences your puppy has during their formative months can shape their temperament, behavior, and how they interact with the world for the rest of their lives. While early socialization is crucial, it doesn't end once your puppy reaches a certain age or has met a few new people. Ongoing socialization is essential for maintaining a confident, well-adjusted dog who can handle new experiences and environments. In this section, we'll discuss the importance of continuing socialization, how to do so safely and effectively, and the benefits of puppy classes and group play.

1. The Importance of Exposing Your Puppy to New People, Animals, and Environments Regularly

The more positive experiences your puppy has with different people, animals, and environments, the more comfortable and confident they will be in the world. Socialization helps prevent behavioral problems such as fear or aggression toward new situations, strangers, or other dogs. Ongoing exposure to various stimuli teaches your puppy that new experiences are nothing to fear.

- **Meeting New People**
  It's essential to expose your puppy to a variety of people, including men, women, children, and people of different ages and backgrounds. This exposure helps your puppy become comfortable around diverse individuals and reduces the likelihood of fear or aggression toward unfamiliar people as they grow. Arrange playdates, walks in busy areas, or invite friends and family over to meet your puppy. Always supervise these interactions, especially during the

early stages of socialization, to ensure they are positive experiences.

- **Socializing with Other Animals**
  Interaction with other dogs, as well as animals like cats or farm animals, is important to help your puppy learn proper canine communication and behavior. Puppy parks, dog-friendly cafes, and controlled meetups with other dogs can be great opportunities for your puppy to practice appropriate behavior around their peers. Introduce your puppy to other animals gradually, making sure each interaction is safe and supervised. Positive encounters with other pets can prevent your puppy from developing fear-based behaviors toward animals later on.

- **Exposure to Different Environments**
  Socialization also involves getting your puppy used to different places, sounds, and environments. Take them on car rides, visit parks, and walk through busy streets, public spaces, and quieter areas. Expose them to different surfaces like grass, concrete, and wood floors, as well as different weather conditions. The more environments your puppy experiences early on, the more adaptable and confident they

will be when faced with unfamiliar situations in the future.

2. How to Continue Socializing Your Dog in Safe and Controlled Ways

While ongoing socialization is important, it's equally crucial that these experiences remain positive and stress-free for your puppy. Rushed or poorly managed introductions can result in fear or anxiety, which can be difficult to undo. Here's how to continue socializing your puppy safely and effectively.

- **Take It Slow and Positive Reinforcement**
  Gradual exposure is key. Don't overwhelm your puppy with too much too soon. For example, if you're introducing them to a new dog, make sure the interaction is calm and controlled. Use positive reinforcement to reward calm behavior during socialization, such as praise, treats, or play. This encourages your puppy to associate socialization with good things. Start with low-stress situations and gradually increase the difficulty or complexity of the socialization experience.

- **Watch for Stress Signals**
  Pay attention to your puppy's body language

during socialization. If they seem frightened, stressed, or overly excited, it's important to recognize those signals and take a step back. Signs of stress in puppies may include tail tucking, cowering, excessive barking, or attempts to escape. If your puppy is reacting negatively, give them space, and try again in a different setting or with a more controlled interaction. Continuing socialization in a safe, manageable way ensures that each experience is positive and builds your puppy's confidence.

- **Manage Unwanted Behavior Early**
  If your puppy begins to display signs of fear, aggression, or excessive excitement, address the behavior early by using training techniques like redirection or gentle corrections. For example, if your puppy starts barking at a new dog, you might ask them to "sit" or redirect their attention to you with a treat. Socialization isn't just about exposing your puppy to new things— it's also about helping them learn how to behave appropriately in these situations.

3. The Benefits of Puppy Classes or Group Play for Social Development

Puppy classes or group play sessions can provide structured, safe environments for your puppy to continue their socialization while also learning important life skills. These settings offer valuable opportunities for both you and your puppy to learn together and practice skills in a controlled, supervised manner.

- **Learning in a Structured Setting**
  Puppy classes are designed to teach essential obedience skills while providing socialization opportunities. In these classes, puppies are exposed to a variety of stimuli, including other puppies, new people, and unfamiliar environments, all under the guidance of a professional trainer. This structured setting helps ensure that socialization is done in a safe and positive way, and it provides an opportunity for you to learn how to handle your puppy in a variety of situations.

- **Controlled Group Play for Socialization**
  Group play sessions or puppy meetups are fantastic for giving your puppy the chance to interact with other dogs in a supervised setting.

These sessions allow your puppy to learn proper dog-to-dog communication, such as how to play gently and how to respect another dog's boundaries. For you as the owner, group play provides valuable insights into your puppy's social behavior and gives you the tools to correct any unwanted behavior in real-time.

- **Building Confidence and Positive Associations**

  Puppy classes and group play are not only about learning commands; they are also about building confidence. As your puppy experiences positive interactions with other dogs and people in a structured setting, they begin to associate new experiences with safety and fun. This helps them grow into a well-adjusted, confident adult dog who is comfortable in a variety of social situations.

Conclusion

Continuing socialization is a lifelong process that helps your puppy grow into a confident, well-behaved adult dog. By regularly exposing your puppy to new people, animals, and environments, you create a well-rounded dog who is comfortable in many situations. Keep socialization safe and controlled by taking things slow, watching for stress signals, and using positive reinforcement. Puppy classes and group play offer structured opportunities for your puppy to learn valuable social skills in a supervised setting, further boosting their development. Ongoing socialization not only helps prevent behavioral problems but also strengthens the bond between you and your puppy, setting the foundation for a happy and well-adjusted dog.

Celebrating Success

Training a puppy can feel like a long journey, but every small milestone is a victory worth celebrating. Whether it's learning a new command, overcoming a behavioral hurdle, or simply showing more confidence in public spaces, every step forward is a testament to the hard work you and your puppy have put in. Celebrating success not only reinforces your puppy's positive behaviors but also strengthens the bond between you both. In this section, we'll discuss how to celebrate your puppy's accomplishments, the long-term rewards of consistent training, and how to enjoy the rewarding bond you've built through the process.

1. How to Celebrate Your Puppy's Milestones and Accomplishments

Celebrating your puppy's successes is an essential part of the training process. Positive reinforcement goes beyond treats and praise—it's about recognizing the effort and reinforcing your puppy's growth.

- **Verbal Praise and Affection**

  One of the simplest and most powerful ways to celebrate your puppy's accomplishments is with enthusiastic verbal praise. Words like "Good job!" or "Well done!" along with a happy tone and gentle petting, will reinforce the behavior you're rewarding. Puppies love attention, and they're motivated by your approval, so make sure to let them know they've done something great!

- **Incorporate Fun Rewards**

  Celebrate milestones by incorporating a fun, special reward, such as extra playtime, a favorite toy, or a new chew treat. If your puppy has successfully learned a new command or mastered a difficult behavior, acknowledge that success by making the reward special. This not only keeps your puppy motivated but also ensures they associate the success with positive, enjoyable experiences.

- **Capture the Moment**
  Take a moment to enjoy the success by capturing the milestone in a photo or video. It's easy to get caught up in the next task, but cherishing these moments creates lasting memories. Plus, looking back at those first "sit" or "stay" moments can remind you of how far you and your puppy have come.

2. The Long-Term Rewards of Consistent Training: From a Well-Behaved Puppy to a Happy, Healthy Adult Dog

The benefits of consistent training stretch far beyond the puppy phase. As you continue to train and reinforce positive behavior, your puppy will grow into a well-adjusted, confident adult dog. The habits and skills they develop early on form the foundation for a lifetime of good behavior.

- **Building Good Habits for Life**
  Consistent training helps your puppy establish good habits early. Whether it's walking politely on a leash, coming when called, or simply being calm and well-mannered at home, these

behaviors will serve your dog throughout their life. As your puppy matures, these positive behaviors become second nature, leading to a more relaxed and enjoyable relationship with your dog.

- **Preventing Behavioral Problems**
  One of the most rewarding aspects of consistent training is the prevention of behavioral issues down the line. A well-trained dog is less likely to develop undesirable behaviors like excessive barking, jumping, or chewing. Consistent, positive reinforcement builds a dog that is not only obedient but also mentally and emotionally healthy, which in turn leads to fewer problem behaviors as they grow older.

- **A Happy, Confident Adult Dog**
  A dog that has been socialized and trained consistently is a happy dog. Training builds your puppy's confidence as they learn to navigate the world with clear boundaries, rules, and rewards. This confidence extends beyond just behavior— it creates a dog who is comfortable in new environments, enjoys meeting new people and dogs, and thrives in various situations. The end

result is a well-rounded, happy adult dog who fits seamlessly into your life and home.

3. How to Enjoy the Bond You've Built with Your Puppy Through Training

Training is not just about teaching your puppy commands—it's about strengthening the relationship between you and your dog. The more time you spend together, the more trust and affection you'll build. This bond is one of the greatest rewards of the training process.

- **Quality Time and Connection**
  Training provides a structured opportunity for quality time with your puppy. Each session— whether it's a 10-minute training exercise or a play-filled reward—creates moments for you and your puppy to connect. These small moments of shared experience not only build obedience but also deepen your relationship. The more you train together, the more your puppy learns to trust you as their leader, and the stronger your bond becomes.

- **Celebrating Growth as a Team**
  Every success in training is a shared accomplishment. As you both grow and progress, you'll feel the satisfaction of having

worked together as a team. Each milestone is a reminder of the patience, consistency, and love you've poured into the process. By celebrating these achievements together, you reinforce the joy of working with your puppy as they become more well-behaved and balanced.

- **Enjoying the Fruits of Your Effort**
  The ultimate reward of training is the ability to enjoy your puppy as a well-behaved companion. Whether it's taking them on calm walks, inviting friends over without worrying about jumping, or simply enjoying quiet time together at home, a well-trained puppy enhances every aspect of life. You'll see that the time and effort you invested in training will come back to you in the form of a peaceful, happy household and a dog who's a true joy to be around.

Conclusion

Training is a journey, and every milestone along the way is worth celebrating. Recognize and reward your puppy's successes with praise, affection, and fun rewards, and know that these moments of accomplishment are just the beginning of a long, rewarding relationship with your dog. Consistent training pays off in the long run by fostering a well-behaved, confident, and happy adult dog. As you continue to enjoy the bond you've built through training, you'll find that the process itself is just as fulfilling as the results. Remember, every step forward, no matter how small, is a victory—and it's worth celebrating!

Staying Motivated and Consistent

Training a puppy requires dedication, patience, and consistency. But just like with any goal, it's easy to get sidetracked or lose motivation, especially when life gets busy. The key to long-term success is finding ways to make training enjoyable for both you and your puppy, keeping the routine consistent, and continuously challenging yourselves as you progress. In this section, we'll explore how to keep training fun and rewarding, tips for staying committed to your 10-minute daily routine, and how to set new challenges as your puppy advances.

1. How to Keep Training Fun and Rewarding for You and Your Puppy

Training doesn't have to feel like a chore! The more fun and rewarding you make it, the more engaged your puppy will be—and the more enjoyable the experience will be for you too. Here's how to keep the training process fun and fresh:

- **Incorporate Play into Training**

  One of the easiest ways to keep training fun is to mix it with play. Use games like fetch, tug-of-war, or hide-and-seek to teach commands or reinforce positive behaviors. For example, you can practice "sit" before throwing a ball or use "stay" during a game of hide-and-seek to improve impulse control. When your puppy associates training with play, they'll look forward to each session.

- **Vary the Rewards**

  Keep your puppy interested by varying the rewards. While treats are a staple in training, don't hesitate to mix things up with other forms of reinforcement like toys, praise, or even extra playtime. A treat might work one day, but a favorite squeaky toy might be more motivating the next. This variety will keep your puppy engaged and prevent the training from feeling too routine.

- **Use Positive Reinforcement**

  Make sure that every training session ends on a positive note, even if things don't go perfectly. When your puppy successfully performs a command, immediately offer them praise, a treat, or affection. Ending on a positive note reinforces the idea that training is fun, and it motivates your puppy to keep trying. Additionally, keeping a positive attitude helps you stay motivated too, as you'll see the progress and enjoy the process.

2. Tips for Staying Committed to a 10-Minute Daily Routine, Even on Busy Days

Life is hectic, and it's easy to let training slip when you're balancing work, errands, family, and other responsibilities. But sticking to your 10-minute daily routine is essential for long-term success. Here are some practical tips for staying committed:

- **Set a Consistent Time Each Day**
  Try to schedule training at the same time each day, even if it's just for a few minutes. Whether it's in the morning before you start work, during your lunch break, or in the evening after dinner, having a set time each day creates a predictable routine for both you and your puppy. Treat it like an appointment that can't be skipped, and you'll be more likely to stick to it.

- **Incorporate Training into Daily Activities**
  Look for opportunities to integrate training into

everyday tasks. You don't always need a dedicated training session to reinforce behaviors. For example, you can practice "sit" and "stay" before meals, or work on leash walking during your daily walk. Even a few seconds here and there can add up over time, and these mini training moments can be just as effective as formal sessions.

- **Use a Training Calendar or Tracker**
  Sometimes it helps to have a visual reminder to stay on track. Use a training calendar or app to keep track of your sessions and mark off each day you complete a 10-minute training routine. It's a small but effective way to hold yourself accountable and celebrate your consistency. Plus, seeing your progress over time is incredibly motivating!

3. Setting New Challenges as Your Puppy Progresses to Keep Training Engaging

As your puppy masters the basics, it's important to keep training engaging and challenging. Continuing to set new goals and challenges will prevent boredom and push your puppy to keep learning. Here's how to keep things fresh:

- **Gradually Increase Difficulty**

  Once your puppy has learned a command, challenge them by increasing the difficulty. For example, if your puppy has mastered "sit" in a quiet room, practice it in a busier environment or with more distractions, like toys or other people around. Gradually increasing the level of difficulty helps your puppy generalize the behavior to different situations and reinforces their learning.

- **Add New Commands or Tricks**

  If your puppy is excelling at basic commands like "sit," "stay," or "come," start introducing new ones. Teaching fun tricks like "shake," "roll over," or "spin" can keep training engaging while also strengthening your puppy's overall obedience. As your puppy grows and matures, you can introduce more advanced skills, such as leash walking without pulling, or even agility training if that interests you both.

- **Challenge Yourself Too**

  Training isn't just about your puppy—it's about you, too! As your puppy becomes more skilled, challenge yourself to refine your own training techniques. Work on being more consistent with your cues, using clearer body language, or practicing training in more challenging environments. By continually challenging both your puppy and yourself, you'll ensure that the training process stays dynamic and rewarding for both of you.

Conclusion

Staying motivated and consistent with your puppy's training doesn't have to be difficult. By making training fun, incorporating it into your daily routine, and setting new challenges as your puppy progresses, you can keep both you and your puppy engaged throughout the training process. Remember, the 10-minute daily routine isn't just about reaching the end goal—it's about the journey of building a strong bond and creating positive experiences together. With a little creativity and commitment, you'll stay on track, and your puppy will continue to thrive!

Tracking Progress

Tracking your puppy's progress throughout their training journey is essential for staying motivated, celebrating successes, and identifying areas for improvement. Whether you're a first-time dog owner or a seasoned trainer, regularly monitoring your puppy's growth can help you adjust your approach as needed and keep both you and your puppy engaged in the learning process. In this section, we'll explore the benefits of tracking your puppy's progress, how to use tools like journals or apps to document achievements, and how to evaluate when it's time to introduce new training goals.

1. The Benefits of Tracking Your Puppy's Training Journey and Celebrating Small Wins

Tracking progress isn't just about recording milestones— it's about recognizing and celebrating your puppy's growth. Celebrating small wins along the way can boost motivation and keep you focused on your ultimate goal: a well-trained, happy puppy. Here's why tracking matters:

- **Celebrates Successes**
  Every new skill or behavior your puppy masters, no matter how small, is a victory worth acknowledging. Tracking allows you to see how far you've come, even on days when it feels like there's little progress. Celebrating small wins— whether it's a successful "sit" on the first try, a calm walk around the block, or your puppy's improvement in crate training—keeps both you

and your puppy motivated and reinforces the positive behaviors you want to see more of.

- **Encourages Consistency**

  When you track your progress, it becomes easier to stay consistent. Seeing that you've been making steady progress over time encourages you to keep up the daily training routine. Plus, when your puppy reaches new goals, you'll feel motivated to continue, knowing that your efforts are paying off.

- **Helps Adjust Expectations**

  Tracking allows you to assess what's working well and where adjustments might be needed. If certain training areas are progressing slower than expected, or if you're noticing a pattern of behavior that needs addressing, tracking helps you evaluate what changes may be necessary. It also ensures that your training goals remain realistic and achievable, helping you avoid frustration and maintain a positive training experience.

2. Using a Journal or App to Track Achievements and Areas for Improvement

A journal or app can be a helpful tool in monitoring your puppy's training progress. These tools not only provide a clear record of your puppy's growth but also give you an easy way to reflect on what's working and what needs more attention. Here's how you can use them effectively:

- **Track Key Behaviors and Commands**
  Create a simple list or chart of the key behaviors and commands you're working on with your puppy (e.g., "sit," "stay," "come"). After each training session, note your puppy's progress for each command. For example, did they respond well to "sit" when distracted by noise or movement? Are they holding the "stay" command for longer periods? This will help you track which behaviors need more practice and which are on track.

- **Log Frequency and Duration of Sessions**
  Keeping track of how often and how long you're training each day can help ensure you stay on top of your 10-minute daily routine. You might want to track the frequency of sessions, how long they lasted, and whether you did additional

training during walks or playtime. This will help you identify any gaps in your routine or days when you've missed training, so you can stay consistent and adjust if needed.

- **Use an App for Easy Tracking**
  If you prefer something more tech-savvy, there are several puppy training apps available that allow you to log your puppy's progress, set training goals, and track behaviors. Some apps even have built-in reminders, tracking charts, and videos to help guide your training sessions. Apps like "Pupford" or "GoodPup" are great tools to stay organized and motivated, allowing you to quickly see where your puppy is excelling and where additional focus is needed.

3. How to Evaluate When It's Time to Introduce New Training Goals

As your puppy masters basic commands and behaviors, it's important to evaluate when to introduce new goals or more advanced training. If your puppy is consistently meeting their current objectives, it may be time to challenge them with new skills or higher levels of complexity. Here's how to assess when to take the next step:

- **Mastery of Basic Commands**

  One sign it's time to introduce new goals is when your puppy consistently responds well to the basic commands you've been focusing on, even in distracting environments. For example, if your puppy has mastered "sit," "stay," and "come" in a quiet room, it's time to start practicing in busier environments, or introduce additional commands like "heel" or "leave it." Mastery of basics often leads naturally to a desire to progress.

- **Improvement in Behavior and Focus**

  If your puppy is showing improved focus, patience, and self-control, this indicates that they're ready for more advanced training. If they can hold a "stay" for longer periods or ignore distractions more easily, you can increase the level of difficulty in your training. Introducing new goals or advanced behaviors will challenge them to continue developing their skills.

- **Identifying New Areas for Development**

  As your puppy grows, new behavioral needs may arise, such as learning to be calm around other dogs or understanding boundaries within your home. Tracking progress can help you spot new challenges that may require attention. If your puppy is excelling at basic training but displaying issues with more specific behaviors— like barking at strangers or chewing furniture— these can be new goals to address in your training sessions.

Conclusion

Tracking your puppy's progress not only keeps you focused but also ensures that you stay on the right path throughout your training journey. By celebrating small wins, using journals or apps to log progress, and knowing when it's time to introduce new goals, you'll ensure that your puppy's training remains engaging, effective, and rewarding. Every step forward, no matter how small, is a victory. Tracking your progress helps you see just how far you've come and motivates you to keep going toward the ultimate goal: a happy, well-trained puppy.

Balancing Life and Training

Life with a new puppy is a whirlwind of excitement, challenges, and, yes, a lot of responsibility. For busy people and families, finding time to train a puppy can feel like a daunting task, especially when juggling work, errands, social commitments, and everything else that comes with daily life. But the good news is that with a little planning and flexibility, training can seamlessly fit into your busy routine. In this section, we'll explore how to integrate training into your daily life, balance it with fun and bonding activities, and make the most of short, frequent training sessions to ensure your puppy thrives without overwhelming your schedule.

1. How to Seamlessly Integrate Training into Your Daily Routine, Even with a Busy Lifestyle

Training doesn't have to take up hours of your day—it can be seamlessly woven into the fabric of your routine, making it a natural part of everyday life. Here's how:

- **Maximize Small Moments**

  Training doesn't require a dedicated block of time every day. Look for small, opportune moments throughout your day to reinforce basic behaviors. For example, practice "sit" before your puppy gets their meal, or "stay" while you put on their leash before a walk. These quick, everyday moments are the perfect opportunities to reinforce your puppy's training without disrupting your schedule.

- **Pair Training with Other Activities**

  You can integrate training into existing activities.

For instance, while you're waiting for your coffee to brew or watching TV, work on simple commands like "sit," "down," or "shake." During walk times, use the opportunity to practice leash training or "heel." The key is pairing training with everyday actions that you already do, so it doesn't feel like an added task.

- **Use a Timer for Quick Sessions**
  With just 10 minutes a day, training can easily be squeezed in, even during the busiest of days. Set a timer for your training sessions, and use those few minutes to focus entirely on your puppy. A quick, concentrated burst of training is just as effective—if not more so—than long, drawn-out sessions. Whether it's before work, during lunch, or before bed, a short training window fits into your schedule without overwhelming you.

2. Balancing Training with Quality Bonding Time and Fun Activities

While training is important, it's also crucial to maintain a balance between work and play. The bond you share with your puppy is built not just through commands and structure, but through quality time spent together. Here's how to ensure training is a positive, enjoyable part of your day, while also making time for fun and relaxation:

- **Incorporate Play into Training**
  Training doesn't have to be all work and no play! Make training a fun and interactive experience by incorporating play into your sessions. Use fetch, tug-of-war, or hide-and-seek to reinforce commands and build excitement. This keeps your puppy engaged and ensures they enjoy learning, while also providing you both with time for fun, positive interactions. Playtime is a great way to strengthen your bond while also reinforcing behaviors.

- **Quality Time, Not Quantity**
  It's not about how much time you spend with your puppy—it's about the quality of that time. Even if you're busy, a few minutes of focused attention and positive reinforcement can go a long way in building trust and strengthening your relationship. Spend time just sitting with your puppy, petting them, or engaging in calm activities like cuddling or interactive play. These moments of connection are just as important for your puppy's well-being as formal training sessions.

- **Plan Family Activities Around Training**
  If you have a family, make training a group activity. Get everyone involved in short sessions, whether it's working on "sit" with the kids or practicing leash walking with your partner. Incorporating family members into training not only keeps everyone accountable but also strengthens the bond between your puppy and your household. Balance training with fun family activities—whether it's a dog-friendly outing or a walk to the park—to ensure your puppy enjoys both work and play.

3. How Short, Frequent Training Sessions Can Fit into Any Schedule, Without Overwhelming Your Day

One of the main principles of this book is that training doesn't have to be time-consuming. With just 10 minutes a day, you can make meaningful progress without adding stress to your busy life. Here's how to make the most of short, frequent training sessions:

- **Focus on 10-Minute Sessions**
  The beauty of short training sessions is that they're easy to fit into your day, even if you have a packed schedule. Instead of trying to carve out

long chunks of time, dedicate just 10 minutes each day to focused training. You can split these sessions into smaller intervals if needed—two or three 3- to 5-minute sessions throughout the day work just as well as one longer block. The key is consistency. Regular, short sessions are more effective than long, infrequent ones.

- **Train During Downtime**
  Take advantage of moments when you're not doing anything else to incorporate training. For example, while you're watching TV, waiting for dinner to cook, or during a lull in your workday, spend a few minutes reinforcing basic commands or practicing tricks. These natural pauses in your day provide perfect opportunities to engage with your puppy without disrupting your routine.

- **Keep Sessions Focused and Fun**
  Short training sessions are ideal for keeping both you and your puppy engaged. Aim for focused, goal-oriented sessions with clear objectives— such as practicing "sit," "stay," or "come"—and always end on a positive note. Quick training sessions help prevent both you and your puppy from feeling overwhelmed, ensuring that

training remains a fun and rewarding experience, rather than a burden.

Conclusion

Balancing life and training with a busy schedule doesn't have to be stressful or overwhelming. By integrating short, frequent training sessions into your daily routine, finding opportunities to bond and play, and staying committed to a 10-minute daily routine, you can ensure that both you and your puppy thrive. Remember, consistency is key, and even the smallest moments of training can make a big impact over time. With a little creativity and planning, you'll be able to raise a happy, well-trained puppy while still managing your busy lifestyle.

To Conclude Your Puppy Training Journey

Congratulations! You've reached the end of *Puppy Training in 10 Minutes a Day*. By now, you have all the tools, techniques, and strategies to transform your puppy into a well-behaved, happy, and healthy companion—all within just 10 minutes a day. This book has shown you that training doesn't have to be a time-consuming or overwhelming task, especially when you break it down into short, consistent sessions that fit into your busy lifestyle.

The Importance of Puppy Training

Puppy training is not just about teaching your dog commands—it's about building a lifelong bond of trust, understanding, and communication. A well-trained puppy is not only a joy to live with, but it also fosters a strong, positive relationship between you and your pet. Through consistent, positive reinforcement, you've set the foundation for a harmonious household, where both you and your puppy understand each other's needs and expectations.

Remember, training isn't just a phase; it's an ongoing journey. As your puppy grows and matures, so too will their skills and behavior. The principles you've learned in this book—like consistency, positive reinforcement, short sessions, and integrating training into daily life—will continue to serve you well, making puppy training an effortless part of your routine, no matter how busy life gets.

Let's Review What We Learned

Throughout *Puppy Training in 10 Minutes a Day*, we've covered everything from the importance of early training and socialization, to the power of consistency, setting realistic goals, and creating a routine that works for your lifestyle. You've learned how to teach essential commands like "sit," "stay," and "come" using simple, effective methods, and how to incorporate training into your daily life without overwhelming yourself. We've explored how to use positive reinforcement, how to stay motivated and consistent, and even how to make training fun and engaging for both you and your puppy.

The key takeaway? Consistency and patience—along with a commitment to 10-minute daily training sessions—will give you the results you desire, and create a joyful, well-adjusted puppy who is ready to be your best companion. Training doesn't need to be perfect or take hours of your time. It just needs to be intentional, and you've already set yourself up for success by following the steps laid out in this book.

Thank You for Reading

I want to take a moment to thank you for reading *Puppy Training in 10 Minutes a Day* from start to finish. You've invested time and energy into making your life with your puppy more rewarding, and that commitment will pay off in countless ways. I'm so proud of you for taking this important step in your puppy's development, and I'm confident that you'll continue to see the positive results of your efforts in the days, weeks, and months ahead.

I know training a puppy can be a lot of work, but I also know that it can be incredibly fulfilling—and with the tools and strategies you now have at your disposal, I'm sure you and your puppy will have an amazing time learning and growing together.

I would love to hear from you!

If this book has helped you, I'd love to hear about it! Please consider leaving a review on Amazon to share your experience with others who may be looking for a similar resource. Your feedback not only helps me improve but also helps other puppy owners find the guidance they need. Every review, big or small, makes a difference, and I truly appreciate you taking the time to share your thoughts. Also, as a thank you you can receive a Puppy Puzzles gift for joining our mailing list where you will find out about other future dog-related materials to help you on the journey.

Scan code below with mobile device:

Amazon Review

Puppy Puzzles Gift

Final Thoughts

You've got this! Thank you again for reading, and I wish you and your puppy many happy and successful training sessions ahead.

With gratitude, love and best wishes,

Andre St Pierre

References

American Kennel Club (AKC). (n.d.). *Puppy training tips*. Retrieved from https://www.akc.org/expert-advice/training/puppy-training-tips/

American Veterinary Society of Animal Behavior (AVSAB). (2018). *Position statement on puppy socialization*. Retrieved from https://avsab.org/

Association of Professional Dog Trainers (APDT). (n.d.). *Dog training resources*. Retrieved from https://apdt.com/

Fenzi, N. (2015). *Train the Dog: Training Exercises for Both You and Your Dog*. Dogwise Publishing.

Houpt, K. A. (2005). *Domestic Animal Behavior for Veterinarians and Animal Scientists*. Wiley-Blackwell.

Horwitz, D. F., & Mills, D. S. (Eds.). (2009). *Behavioral Issues in Companion Animals: A Guide for Veterinary Practitioners*. Wiley-Blackwell.

McConnell, P. (2002). *The Other End of the Leash: Why We Do What We Do Around Dogs*. Ballantine Books.

Overall, K. L. (2013). *Manual of Clinical Behavioral Medicine for Dogs and Cats*. Elsevier Health Sciences.

Pryor, K. (1999). *Don't Shoot the Dog: The New Art of Teaching and Training*. Bantam Books.

Humane Society of the United States (HSUS). (n.d.). *Puppy training basics*. Retrieved from https://www.humanesociety.org/resources/puppy-training-basics

Printed in Great Britain
by Amazon